Fair Ladies

Renaissance and Baroque Studies and Texts

Eckhard Bernstein
General Editor

Vol. 9

PETER LANG
New York • San Francisco • Bern • Baltimore
Frankfurt am Main • Berlin • Wien • Paris

Katherine J. Roberts

Fair Ladies

Sir Philip Sidney's Female Characters

PETER LANG
New York • San Francisco • Bern • Baltimore
Frankfurt am Main • Berlin • Wien • Paris

Library of Congress Cataloging-in-Publication Data

Roberts, Katherine J.
   Fair ladies: Sir Philip Sidney's female characters / Katherine J.
Roberts.
      p.   cm. — (Renaissance and baroque studies and texts; vol. 9)
   Includes bibliographical references.
    1. Sidney, Philip, Sir, 1554–1586—Characters—Women. 2. Women
and literature—England—History—16th century. 3. Women—
England—History—Renaissance, 1450–1600. I. Title. II. Series.
   PR2343.R58   1993   821'.3—dc20   93-20209
   ISBN 0-8204-2145-6   CIP
   ISSN 0897-7836

Die Deutsche Bibliothek-CIP-Einheitsaufnahme
Roberts, Katherine J.:
Fair ladies: Sir Philip Sidney's female characters / Katherine J.
Roberts. - New York; Bern; Berlin; Frankfurt /M.; Paris;
Wien: Lang, 1993
   (Renaissance and baroque studies and texts; Vol. 9)
   ISBN 0-8204-2145-6
NE: GT

#27432419

Cover design by James F. Brisson.

The paper in this book meets the guidelines for permanence and
durability of the Committee on Production Guidelines for
Book Longevity of the Council on Library Resources.

© Peter Lang Publishing, Inc., New York 1993

Printed in the United States of America.

Table of Contents

Acknowledgments

I am most grateful to the following people for their help in completing this book: Dr. Margaret Arculus, without whom this book would never have been formulated; Dr. Robert Turner and Dr. Roger Sundell, both of whom gave me significant guidance; Barbara Skeans, who encouraged my endeavor from the first; Bruce and Kirsti Kokko and the Saturday Night Study Group which gave me moral support; Dr. Heidi Burns, my editor, who also became my friend; my children, Laura and Jeff Roberts, who may have suffered the most; and my husband, Ronald E. Roberts, who gave me the idea in the first place and then encouraged and supported me through every step of the process.

The translation of Petrarch's Sonnet XVI was reprinted by permission from *Petrarch: Selected Poems*, translated by Anthony Mortimer, copyright 1977, The University of Alabama Press.

Social and Literary Images of Women

A close examination of Sir Philip Sidney's three major works, the *Old Arcadia*, *Astrophil and Stella*, and the *New Arcadia*, reveals that his female characters become increasingly complex as he departs more and more from existing social and literary models of women. Courtesy books, secular handbooks written to teach women how to conduct themselves in almost any situation, effectively reveal the concepts about women that prevailed in Elizabethan society. Many of these books were written for specific women, but some, like Vives' *Instruction for a Christian Woman* written for Catherine of Aragon in 1523, were reprinted many times and used by a much wider audience for the general education of women. Although they do not necessarily reflect the way women acted, thought, or were treated, they do demonstrate a general acceptance of the ideas expressed because they all deliver similar messages about women. Courtesy books illustrate the contemporary concepts of the Ideal Woman, which changed surprisingly little from Geoffrey de la Tour-Landry writing for his daughters in 1372 to Juan Luis Vives writing in 1523. These handbooks for women also illustrate the current concepts of the frailties of women—the natural vices the writers thought women must constantly battle. Two opposing images of women emerge from these books: the saint and the whore. The saint embodies all of the virtues that a patriarchal society desired in women: piety, obedience, humility, silence, and most importantly, chastity; the whore exhibits all of the vices that woman's frail and inferior nature develops if left unrestrained: lust, deceit, pride, boldness, and the desire to rule men. The writers of these books cautioned women to be on guard constantly in order to preserve their virtue, and, as important as virtue itself, the appearance of virtue; even the appearance of failure or weakness in one area was understood to indicate weakness in all.

Secular conduct manuals were also written for men, but they are more diverse than those written for women, since men had many types of occupations; women had only one—marriage. Books written about education for men, like Elyot's *The Boke Named the Governor*, establish ideals for men to strive for, but they generally set out practical courses of study to help men gradually achieve their virtuous goals, which were usually directed toward public action. Men were expected to grow into virtue, and if they stumbled along the way, they could retrace their steps and start over. Writers for women demanded perfection from the start; a woman was not allowed to slip. Perhaps this is because the virtues required of women involve a negation of self, while those required of men promote the development and enlargement of the self. Elyot himself compares the desired virtues of men and women. He states that "A man in his natural perfection is fierce, hardy, strong in opinion, covetous of glory, desirous of knowledge, appetiting by generation to bring forth his semblable," and adds that "The good nature of a woman is to be mild, timorous, tractable, benign, of sure remembrance, and shamefast" (77-78). Ruth Kelso points out that "The moral ideal for the lady is essentially Christian...as that for the gentleman is essentially pagan. For him the ideal is self-expansion and realization....For the lady the direct opposite is prescribed. The eminently Christian virtues of chastity, humility, piety, and patience under suffering and wrong are the necessary virtues" (36). Since women's virtues depend on the negation of self, any sign of self-will in one area could lead to failure in all areas; perhaps this is the reason that courtesy books for women tend to paint them as either black or white, a stereotyped depiction in literature. Fiction from Jean de Meun to Ariosto—Sidney's models—perpetuates this striking dichotomy.

In several of Sidney's models, the inferiority of women breaks through the heroine's overlay of virtue in one way or another. Otherwise virtuous women often exhibit relatively minor faults like the jealousy and feminine deceit that prove their natural inferiority to the heroes. Thus, the heroines, no matter how much they strive toward virtue, demonstrate their need for the masculine guidance of father or husband. Submission to a superior male is the solution to woman's weak nature, and each acquired virtue counteracts a natural vice that must be subdued. Authors such as Lisa Jardine, writing about Shakespeare's heroines (*Still Harping on*

Daughters), and Katherine Usher Henderson and Barbara F. McManus, writing about the *querrelle des femmes* (*Half Humankind*), as well as others, group women's stereotypical characteristics under headings of recognizable character types like the seductress and the shrew. This kind of grouping is useful if the works under examination contain these character types. Sidney, however, uses the contemporary notions of female virtue and vice in combinations that do not fit the usual patterns of character types. I will therefore examine these virtues and vices separately, first as they appear in courtesy books, and then as they appear in Sidney's literary models, in order to demonstrate Sidney's deviation from stereotypes and his portrayal of women as individuals.

I

The Book of the Knight of the Tower was written in 1372 by Geoffrey de la Tour-Landry for the instruction of his three daughters (Bornstein 134). William Caxton translated it into English and printed it in 1484. This virulent book strongly represents the failings of women. To balance it there is *The Goodman of Paris*, written by an elderly man for his young bride sometime between 1392 and 1395 (*Goodman* 1). The Goodman expresses many of the same ideas as the Knight of the Tower, but he is much more compassionate in his approach and much less insistent on the natural depravity of women. Two books by Christine de Pisan, *The book of the City of Ladies* and *The Treasure of the City of Ladies*, both written around 1405, reflect a woman's point of view. Juan Luis Vives' *Instruction of a Christian Woman*, written in 1523 at the request of Catherine of Aragon for the instruction of her daughter Mary Tudor, represents humanistic Renaissance ideas. Vives was reprinted approximately thirty-six times in England and elsewhere, in at least six languages, by the end of the sixteenth century (Wayne 15). *The Book of the Courtier* by Baldessare Castiglione, widely acclaimed in Elizabethan times, is an instruction book for courtiers. Although written mainly for men, *The Courtier* also describes the proper conduct of the gentlewoman. These books, written across a wide range of time for a variety of reasons by people from various walks of life, present many of the same ideas, indicating how embedded they were in the culture.[1]

One commonly expressed idea is that the vices are natural to women; the virtues may be acquired by constant suppression (by the woman and by the men who control her) of the vices. In *Renaissance Notions of Women*, Ian Maclean says that medieval and Renaissance men thought a woman's "assumed frailty of body, which best befits her for the care of young and makes her unsuited to exposure to the dangers of the outside world, is accompanied by mental and emotional weaknesses that are the natural justification for her exclusion from public life, responsibility, and moral fulfillment" (43-44). Maclean explains that in Renaissance medical theory,

> Woman is considered to be inferior to man in that the psychologi-
> cal effects of her cold and moist humours throw doubt on her
> control of her emotions and her rationality; furthermore, her less
> robust physique predisposes her, it is thought, to a more protected
> and less prominent role in the household and in society. (46)

Renaissance medical theory also postulates that women's natural humors make women more changeable, which results in deceit, inconstancy, and infidelity. Further, the uterus adds to the deleterious psychological effects of the humours. It "weakens rationality and increases the incidence and violence of passions in women: hate, vengeance, fear, anger are all thought commonly to hold greater sway over the female sex; but also pity and love" (Maclean 42). Patriarchal society presumed the inferiority of women, and medical science diligently tried to discover the causes for it; everything that made women different from men could be cited as a justification for female inferiority, since to be male was to be superior. If women are softer than men, then softness is inferior; if women cry more than men, then crying is inferior. The idea that a woman is a mistake in nature's efforts to produce a superior, or male, product was generally abandoned during the Renaissance[2]; instead, the female was declared "equally perfect in her sex" (Maclean 44). However, medical scientists generally agreed that woman's humours and physiology make her inferior to man (44). The perfection of the female sex as a biological phenomenon did not make females equal to males; in the hierarchy of living creatures, woman ranked below man, and courtesy books written for the instruction of women make that inequality very clear.

The first virtue that writers of courtesy books in the Middle Ages speak of is piety, perhaps because they consider piety to be the foundation on which all other virtues depend. Geoffrey de la Tour-Landry in *The Book of the Knight of the Tower* describes attention to religious duties as a kind of talisman that will protect his daughters from their natural weaknesses. He instructs them in practices that will contribute to their piety, like fasting (17), keeping the eyes downcast (25), charity (37), and moderation in dress (38). He illustrates his instructions with stories of women who, because they did not follow pious ritual, fell into sin and were punished. One such story, concerned with specific rituals of prayer, describes the behavior of two daughters of the Emperor of Constantinople; one spent much time in prayer for the souls of the dead, but the other scorned her sister for these practices. The two daughters meet knights, and succumbing to temptation, invite the knights "to come to them pryvely by nyght" (15). The prayers of the pious daughter protect her, because the souls of the dead men she prayed for rise up to prevent her knight from coming to her. The other sister meets with her lover, however, and becomes pregnant. The emperor has both the girl and her lover put to death (15). Since she has not gone through the motions necessary to acquire her talisman, she has no protection from her natural tendencies and her frail spirit.

Not all medieval writers of courtesy books had such a limited concept of women. The Goodman of Paris and Christine de Pisan also encourage piety, but they do not believe that religious rituals magically protect women from their natural inclinations to sin; they rather favor true devotion to God. Christine is also aware of the importance of appearances to the reputations of her readers; she advocates true piety as self-defense—a way women can protect their good names.

Although they do not generally contain long discussions of piety, Renaissance courtesy books assume it to underlie all other virtues (Kelso 26). In his *Instructions of a Christian Woman*, Vives makes the assumption that his readers desire to please God above all else. In his list of books suitable for unmarried girls in their formative years, he urges parents to give their daughters religious material to read in order to occupy their minds and keep them from "thinking on armour, and tourney and man's valiance" (57). He recommends the Gospels, Acts, the Epistles, the Old Testament, and such early church fathers as Jerome, Augustine, and Hilary (62).[3] Vives further believes that a girl must comprehend the meaning of her prayers: "I would she should understand what she prayeth, or else speak in that language that she doth understand. Whatsoever she prayeth in Latin, let her get it declared to her in her own tongue" (89). This advice is important because it demonstrates that Vives believed girls to be rational. Piety is also the underlying principle for obedience; girls are to love God first, and their parents next. To their parents, daughters should "neither show in mind, countenance, nor gesture any stubbornness but reckon them to be as it were a very image of almighty God, the father of all thing[s]" (108). Thus, obedience to God leads to obedience to parents, a commonplace of hierarchical reasoning.

Writers of courtesy books hoped that piety would help to counteract that most feared of all the vices natural to women: lust. Medical opinion at this time concerning women provided some foundation for the widespread belief in women's naturally lecherous tendencies. The uterus was blamed for "excessive desire for coitus" in women (Maclean 41). In fact, "Frequent sexual intercourse, according to medical opinion, was necessary for female health, for without it the uterus might dry up" (Brundage 376). Thus, a woman's uterus leads her into natural and uncontrollable lust, and female sexual desires had to be strongly restrained.[4] Because women were perceived as naturally lecherous, most courtesy books—if not all—emphasize chastity. While men derived honor from doing great deeds, women's honor derived from remaining chaste. Even the gentle Goodman of Paris feels that he must tell his wife what will become of her reputation if she is not chaste:

> All good is departed from maid or woman who faileth in virginity,
> continence and chastity: not riches, not beauty, not good sense, nor
> high lineage, nor any other merit can ever wipe out the ill fame of
> the opposite vice, above all if in a woman it be once committed,
> in soothe if it be but suspected, wherefore many wise women have
> kept themselves not only from the deed but from the suspicion
> thereof, in purpose to win the name of virginity.... (94)

Later he adds that "even supposing that she be wrongly suspected, never can that ill fame be wiped away" (105). For the Goodman to speak this strongly about chastity demonstrates the social importance of this virtue.

Christine de Pisan assumes that women will be chaste, so she does not teach them about chastity. Instead, she advises her readers not to appear unchaste. She says specifically that a princess will have chastity "so abundantly...that in neither word nor deed, appearance, ornaments, nor bearing, conduct, social pomp nor expression will there be anything for which she could be criticized" (*Treasure* 59). She gives special advice to ladies of the court because they will meet men socially: "You must be in your manner, speech and all actions not too familiar nor intimate with men" (110). They must take more care than others to guard their reputations, since they will be more observed than other women. She advises women that friendships with men will fuel gossip and make other men think that the ladies are not virtuous, which could lead to attempted seductions (115).

Baldessare Castiglione describes the ideal gentlewoman as one capable of entertaining courtiers with her lively conversation (217), but adds that she must clothe herself in "a kinde of goodnes, that she may be esteamed no less chaste, wise and courteise, then pleasant...and therfore must she kepe a certein meane very harde, and...dirived of contrary matters, and come just to certein limites, but not passe them" (217). Castiglione, like Christine, assumes that his perfect lady will be chaste—after all, he is creating her—but she, like the ladies Christine addresses, must be very careful to avoid the slightest appearance of fault: "She ought to be ...circumspect and to take...heed that she give no occasion to be yll reported of, and so to beehave her selfe, that she be not onlye not spotted wyth anye fault, but not so much as with suspicion" (216). One of Castiglione's speakers explains why: "...we oure selves [men] have established for a lawe, that in us wanton life is no vice, nor default, nor anye sclaunder, and in women it is so great a reproche and shame, that she that hath once an yll name, whether the report that goith of her be true or false, hathe loste her credit for ever" (199). For Castiglione, chastity is the foundation of women's honor; without that virtue, she has none.

Vives is even more explicit about the lady's reputation. In fact, most of his teaching in *The Instruction of a Christian Woman* focuses on chastity and the appearance of chastity. Pamela Joseph Benson, in her book *The Invention of the*

Renaissance Woman, calls Vives "a restrictor and repressor whose insistence on the primacy of the single virtue of chastity created a very narrow field of activity for women" (172). Indeed, in his preface Vives observes that although there are many precepts for men because they have much to do at home and abroad, a woman "hath no charge to see to but her honesty and chastity. Wherefore when she is informed of that she is sufficiently appointed" (34). Parents must keep a close watch on their daughter from her infancy "lest any spot of vice stick on her" (41). He advises parents to keep their baby daughter from all men so that she will not develop the tendency to love them in her youth. This is especially important because "love is the most strong in women because they be most disposed to pleasure and dalliance" (47). Older girls must be simply clothed so they will not be tempted to go out and show off their rich apparel to men. He draws on antiquity as his source for this advice: "Plutarch saith that it is a custom in Egypt that women should wear no shoes, because they should abide at home. Likewise if thou take from women silk, and cloth of gold and silver, precious stones, and gems, thou shalt the more easily keep them at home" (79). Vives implies that the only woman a husband or father can trust is one in complete seclusion, isolated from temptation.

Throughout *The Instruction of a Christian Woman* Vives speaks of woman's frailty, stressing the idea that girls must be more strictly tended than boys in order to counteract their weak natures. He wants girls to be occupied at all times with handwork or reading virtuous books so that they are never idle because "A woman's mind is unstable and abideth not long in one place. It falleth from the good to bad without any labour" (86). He advises parents not to show too much love to either sons or daughters, but especially daughters, "for they be so set upon pleasures and fantasies, that except they be well bridled and kept under, they run headlong into a thousand mischiefs" (132-133). Clearly, the purpose of Vives' work is to counteract nature. He firmly believes that vice is natural to children, but that girls are more difficult to train than boys; virtues must be forced into them. He notes, too, that society demands more virtue from women than it does from men:

No doubt much more diligence ought to be given about the daughters, that nothing blot their demureness, chastity or sadness, because these things be required more perfect in a woman than a man. (134)

If Vives gives this advice to a queen, Catharine of Aragon, as she raises her daughter, Princess Mary, he must be writing from ideas about women generally accepted in his age; since his work was so widely used, he not only reflected the prevailing theories about women, he perpetuated them.

Although lust was the vice most feared, another vice writers of courtesy books considered natural to women was the desire to dominate men, whether husbands or lovers. This belief led these authors to insist on obedience. Silence and humility are the two virtues that most often accompany obedience in the courtesy literature, since it was commonly thought that women's greatest weapons in the battle for dominance were a sharp tongue and inordinate pride. "The subservience of women was considered the natural state of things rather than a mere social reality. The disorderly, dominant woman was a symbol of chaos" (Bornstein 118). From very early childhood, girls were trained to be obedient to their parents, to do instantly, without question, and silently whatever was demanded of them. A girl would move then from one master, her father, to another, her husband, schooled in obedience, silence, and humility. The Knight of the Tower speaks very strongly to his daughters about the need for obedience to their husbands. He tells his daughters a story about a wife who spoke to her husband "noiously and shamefully to fore the peple" (35). Her husband "bad her ones or twyse, that she shold be stylle and leve," and when she persisted, he "smote her with his fyste to the erthe And smote her with his foote on the vysage so that he brake her nose/ by whiche she was ever after al disfygured" (35). The Knight does not approve of the wife's actions, and he does not censure the husband at all; the husband had the right, indeed the duty, to discipline his wife for her disobedience, as well as for her unruly tongue. According to the Knight of the Tower, obedience requires silence. He cautions his daughters to be silent and submissive, even if their husbands take mistresses. He uses the story of a woman he calls his aunt as an example of obedience in this situation. He says that his aunt's husband actually kept other women in their house, and he often left his wife's bed to go to them.

The wife's silent suffering eventually won the husband back, when loud complaining would have antagonized him. The Knight of the Tower, who is so concerned for his daughters' chastity, recognizes that husbands probably would not be faithful to their wives, and he also recognizes that wives, in reality, had no recourse but to submit; thus, he advises his daughters to endure to these situations quietly and humbly and wait for their husbands to repent.

The Goodman of Paris was also concerned about his wife's submission, although he did not try to frighten her into obedience with threats of violence. He speaks to his wife about obedience in a paternal tone, kind but strict. He quotes one of the many versions of the Patient Griselda story to illustrate perfect wifely obedience, although he does add that he thinks this trial carries the test too far (137). The Goodman also mentions other tests of wifely obedience less difficult than Griselda's, but which wives failed because they were too proud to obey what they considered strange or trivial commands from their husbands. In one of these examples, three abbots and three husbands devised such a test to see if wives or monks would be more obedient. Each gave a command without explanation, the abbots that each monk should "leave his room open and rod beneath his pillow, and await the discipline that his abbot was in mind to give him," and the husbands that their wives should "set and leave a broom behind the door of their room all night long" (153). The monks obeyed, but the wives did not. The Goodman's belief in the natural inferiority of women shows through his explanation of these results:

> Thus the monks were obedient in a greater thing to their abbotts, which is a marvel; but it is natural, for they be men; and the wedded women were less obedient in a less thing and to their own husbands, that should have been their special care, for 'twas their nature, since they were women.... (154-155)

Even the kind and wise Goodman subscribed to the notion that women were not as capable of virtue as men. This story illustrates the Goodman's admonition to his wife to obey even the most trivial of her husband's commands. This kind of blind and unreasoning obedience required the wife's complete trust in her husband as superior, abbot to her monk.

The Goodman also instructs his wife to be silent: "You should be silent or at least temperate in speech and wise to keep and to hide your husband's secrets" (179). This advice he repeats several times, once telling his wife not to reveal her husband's vices or sins, and then telling her to "conquer your woman's nature, which is such (so it is said) that they—to wit the bad and wicked ones—can hide nothing" (180). Although the Goodman tempers his criticism of women by limiting it to "the bad and wicked ones," he reveals in his repeated warnings his concern about the natural tendency of women to talk too much. He tells his wife the story of the child Papirius who listened one day in the Roman senate, and, like the senators, was sworn to secrecy. When he got home, his mother badgered him to tell her what went on. Not willing to reveal the truth, he swore his mother to secrecy and told her a lie. His mother promptly spread the lie until it came back to the senators, and it was revealed that a young boy was better able to keep secrets than a grown woman (180-182). The Goodman clearly believed not only in women's uncontrollable loquaciousness but also in their childish nature.

This belief in women's infantile nature provides one rationale for the insistence on their submission to men in courtesy literature. The laws of England in the Middle Ages and the Renaissance demonstrate that women were considered as irresponsible as children, and, like children, required guardianship. Therefore, the laws gave custody of women to their fathers and husbands. The law made wives completely dependent on their husbands in most cases. *The Laws Respecting Women*, printed in 1777, is a compilation of laws concerning women that were unchanged from the time of the Magna Charta until the publication date. One precept about the status of women occurs over and over again:

> By marriage the very being or legal existence of a woman is suspended; or at least it is incorporated and consolidated into that of the husband; under whose wing, protection and cover, she performs everything.... (65)

The law extends this idea to property that the wife might have owned before the marriage; all that was hers became her husband's:

> By marriage those chattels which belonged to the woman before
> marriage, are by act of law vested in the husband, with the same
> powers as the wife when sole had over them; and this is founded
> on the notion of an unity of person subsistent between the husband
> and wife; it being held in law that they are one person, so that the
> very being and essence of the woman is suspended during the
> coverture [marriage], or entirely merged and incorporated in that of
> the husband. And hence it follows, that whatever personal property
> belongs to the wife before marriage is thereby absolutely vested in
> the husband. (149)

Thus, legally, except for a very few special cases, the wife had nothing she could call her own "except what she could specifically lay claim to in a marriage contract. By marriage, the husband and wife became one person in law—and that person was the husband" (Stone 195); everything belonged to her husband, including "ready money, jewels, household goods, and the like..." (*The Laws* 151). The wife had no legal existence. She was not even able to make a will because "a married woman is not considered as possessing sufficient liberty to make a will but under certain restrictions and in certain situations" (*The Laws* 178). Generally, widows were the only women who had any control of their own lives.

Christine de Pisan recognized this precarious legal position of women in society and counseled wives to submit to their husbands for their own good. She says that a wife should "love her husband and live in peace with him, or otherwise she will have already discovered the torments of Hell, where there is nothing but violence" (*Treasure* 62). Indeed, beating was considered acceptable discipline for unruly wives.[5] Christine counsels a form of hypocrisy—that a wife should hide her true feelings and appear to accept her husband unconditionally, silently, and without complaint (*Treasure* 62), thus endorsing the virtues of humility, silence and obedience, as do the Goodman and the Knight of the Tower. Like the Knight, Christine describes the possible retribution of an irate husband, but from a somewhat different angle. She advises the wife whose husband has a mistress to ignore the situation if she cannot change it because,

> As a prudent woman, she will think, "If you speak to him harshly
> you will gain nothing, and if he leads you a bad life you will be
> kicking against the spur; he will perhaps leave you, and people will
> mock you all the more and believe shame and dishonour, and it
> may be still worse for you. You must live and die with him what-
> ever he is like." (*Treasure* 64)

Like the Knight and the Goodman, Christine recognizes the husband's supremacy in marriage. Unlike them, she does not see it as a moral supremacy of a superior being over an inferior one; she sees it as an established legal fact over which women have no control, something they have to learn to live with as well as they can.

Christine de Pisan does not speak specifically of a woman's need to cultivate silence in either *The Book of the City of Ladies* or *The Treasure of the City of Ladies*. In *The Book*, she speaks of men who claim that women cannot keep secrets, listing examples from history of women who did keep secrets, like Portia, the wife of Brutus, who tried to persuade her husband not to kill Julius Caesar. Although Brutus would not listen to Portia's sound advice, she did not betray his plan (134-135). Christine uses this story to indicate that women are capable of giving wise counsel, and of being discreet, as well. She asserts that there are many women who are capable of being both, although she maintains that both men and women vary in the strength of all of their virtues (134).[6]

Rather than telling women to maintain silence, Christine advises them to counsel their husbands tactfully in certain situations. A princess, in particular, should speak to her husband on behalf of the people, becoming an intermediary for them (*Treasure* 49). Princesses must also work for the "avoidance of war" (*Treasure* 51). She says that "women are by nature more timid and also of a sweeter disposition [than men], and for this reason, if they are wise and if they wish to, they can be the best means of pacifying men" (*Treasure* 51). Christine recognizes that many women are intelligent, and she asks that they put their abilities humbly at the disposal of their husbands. She says that "the more they humble themselves before their husbands in obedience and reverence, the more their honour will increase" (*Treasure* 138). She speaks rationally of women's constant need to maintain a virtuous reputation, and gives pragmatic advice to her readers to teach them how to cope with the society which they cannot change. In doing so, she actually supports and perpetuates the patriarchal foundations of her society.

There was little alteration in the accepted ideas about women's duty to be obedient to fathers and husbands from the Middle Ages through the Renaissance; Katherine Henderson and Barbara McManus note in *Half Humankind: Contexts and Texts of the Controversy about Women in England 1540-1640* that "all of the domestic conduct books published in England in our period, even those most sympathetic to women, assert the authority of the husband over the wife. Some writers derive this authority from the accounts of the creation and fall in Genesis; others derive it from the intellectual, moral, and physical superiority of men" (77-78). Henderson and McManus further state that *The Homily on Marriage*, which Elizabeth herself caused to be read from the pulpit of the church, "stressed the natural inferiority of women....Like the conduct books, the *Homily* left no doubt that the wife owed her husband unquestioning submission and obedience" (78). Thus, in the Renaissance as well as in the Middle Ages, the dominant wife was considered an abomination. Renaissance writers of conduct books, therefore, placed great emphasis on obedience as a virtue for women to cultivate. Further, as in the Middle Ages, the obedient woman was supposed to be silent; Linda Woodbridge says in *Women and the English Renaissance: Literature and the Nature of Womankind, 1540-1640*, "Women's tongues are instruments of aggression or self-defense; men's are the tools of authority. In either case, speech is an expression of power; but male speech represents legitimate authority, while female speech attempts to usurp authority or rebel against it" (208). In other words, speech is a sign of power and therefore rightfully belongs to men.

Vives strongly promotes the idea that women must be trained to be both obedient and silent. He would have women be silent even with other women: "Full of talk I would not have her, no, not among maids. For as among men to be full of babble I marvel that some regard shame so little, that they do not dispraise it" (99). Vives differs from some other writers of conduct books in that he promotes education for women—but only as a means to train them in the virtues of obedience and silence.[7] Indeed, he hastens to explain that the purpose of educating girls is not to teach them to speak well: "As for eloquence, I have no great care, nor a woman needeth it not, but she needeth goodness and wisdom" (54). He wants women to learn in order to give them something to occupy their minds and to wean them from such light and frivolous pastimes as "songs, dances and such other wanton and peevish plays" (54). Vives would not have girls study the same things that boys study, but only that part of philosophy which improves the disposition (53).

Vives further stipulates that women must not use their learning to teach men, for that would not be in keeping with their inferior state; they may teach only their children or other women:

> For it neither becometh a woman to rule a school nor to live amongst men, or speak abroad...it were better to be at home within and unknown to other folks, and in company to hold her tongue demurely, and let few see her, and none at all hear her. (55)

Thus, women's learning must lead only to silence and submission; women must never feel superior to men. Indeed, Vives believed that a woman's obedience to her husband should extend even beyond the grave; a woman was to be obedient to what she knew of her husband's wishes even after he died, living in seclusion and pious chastity for the rest of her life. Learning would be especially useful in widowhood since one of the most important reasons for women to be educated was to occupy their minds and to keep them from idleness which leads to sin. Yet Vives has no advanced ideas about their capabilities; he rather believes that learning may be one way to counteract their natural weaknesses—to raise them above their sex.

The concepts expressed in the courtesy literature were not new; many had been in existence, perhaps, since Adam blamed Eve for giving him the apple. The conduct books were used to teach girls their proper place and their supportive role in society (Hull 140-143); even conduct books written for men discuss the inferiority of women. Most of the books betray the fear that women will break out of the narrow boundaries established for them to invade the more public spheres of men.[8] The primary boundary was sexual. Writers from Geoffrey de la Tour-Landry to Baldessare Castiglione articulate a sexual double standard for men and women. These writers emphasize that although men may be inconstant or unfaithful, women absolutely must not be. Infidelity in women was a threat to controlled inheritance and primogeniture—the patriarchal foundations of society. Perhaps for this reason, courtesy books illustrate, often very graphically, the evils of women's lust—thus perpetuating the stereotype of the unfaithful wife.

The possibility of female domination was also a threat to male superiority. A dominating wife makes a man subject to ridicule and raucous humor, especially a dominating woman with a sharp tongue—the shrew—who might shame her husband before his peers. The stereotype of the perfect wife as evoked by the courtesy books is chaste and submissive, silent and humble—the self-abasing, silently suffering woman. Many medieval and Renaissance writers of pastoral and romance literature use stereotypes, with few alterations, as their heroines and villainesses.

II

In pastoral and romance, the stereotypically perfect woman— chaste, humble, and silent—becomes the passive, meek heroine with downcast eyes who attracts her lover with her beauty and her blushes of sweet shamefastness. Most heroines stay safely inside castle walls and inspire their lovers to perform great feats of valor in order to win them; these women do very little except give their lovers hope one minute and drive them to the edge of despair the next, revealing their changeable female natures. In romances like Malory's *Morte Darthur* and Ariosto's *Orlando Furioso*, a heroine and her companion may travel through the countryside, generally in search of a champion to right a wrong or perhaps in search of her betrothed who has wandered away to right someone else's wrongs. This usually happens in cases of dire necessity, when the maiden has no nearby knight to champion her, so that, being naturally unable to help herself, she must seek a brave knight to take care of her. The heroine is able to roam the countryside without tarnishing her reputation because she is protected by her virtuous demeanor, her companion, and the knights errant who champion her. In most cases, however, the lovers are the ones risking their lives and building reputations as mighty warriors; the ladies rest in leisured safety, thinking up new tests for their champions. This reversal of roles, with the knight in artificial and voluntary subjection to his lady, occurs only outside of marriage. Ruth Kelso notes that the rules of courtly love made the lover his mistress' slave, while marriage demanded complete submission of the wife to the husband; thus, a lover should probably not marry his mistress, even if he should get the chance, because both would strive for mastery in the marriage (165).[9]

In order to observe the way Sidney's predecessors use cultural stereotypes in the formation of female characters, it is necessary to examine a few representative works which illustrate particular types of literature, especially popular literature, as well as some of the specific models for Sidney's *Arcadia*s. The portion of *Le Roman de la Rose* written by Jean de Meun between 1268 and 1285 is the oldest and one of the most misogynistic of the literary works examined. Controversy about Jean de Meun's work contributed to the *querrelles des femmes* which began in the Middle Ages and continued in the Renaissance. *The Fifteen Joys of Marriage*, probably written by a cleric between 1480 and 1490 (*Fifteen Joys* vii), represents a type of misogynistic literature popular and widespread during the Middle Ages and the Renaissance, a catalogue of faults considered natural to wives that reflects all of the most demeaning stereotypes of women. Chaucer must be included because of the admiration his work excited in the Elizabethan Renaissance; in his *Apologie for Poesie*, Sidney cites him as an authority on the effects of comedy (28). *The Canterbury Tales* incorporate most of the cultural ideas about women—good and bad—expressed in the courtesy literature. Malory's *Morte Darthur* represents popular romance of the Middle Ages, and Ariosto's *Orlando Furioso* and the *Amadis de Gaule*, both cited by Sidney in his *Apologie for Poesie*, represent the more modern versions of popular romance. *The Amadis* and *Orlando Furioso*, along with Sannazzaro's *Arcadia*, Montemayor's *Diana*, and the Hellenic *Aethiopian History* by Heliodorus and *Daphnis and Chloe* by Longus have been cited as possible sources for Sidney's *Arcadia*s.

In these works, whether a woman is good or bad, she rarely plays more than an incidental role in the fiction. The hero is the focus of the story, and the heroine or seductress serves only to point out his virtues and prowess; the heroine generally inspires her lover to heroic action, while the seductress lulls him to indolent inaction. These evil women lead men into sin and softness and strip them of their manhood (actually, love itself, if not restrained by reason, makes men weak and effeminate). The stereotypically feminine vices such villainesses display are lust, deceit, pride, boldness, and the desire to rule men. One major distinction between the portrayal of male and female characters is in their range of behavior; while the female characters always remain either good or evil, heroes, like Ariosto's Ruggiero, may sin and repent several times and never lose their status as heroes.

Medieval and Renaissance fictions rarely mention piety as the source of virtue in their portrayal of women. In fact, authors of these works were apparently more interested in women's vices than their virtues. Evil women are usually much more active in the stories than the heroines, who tend to be boring in their virtuous maidenhood. Lust is the vice most of the villainesses have in common. In *The Fifteen Joys of Marriage*, which ironically warns men not to marry, one character is the wife who takes a lover. Of course, the poor beset husband never has the time or the strength to take a mistress. He is worn out with the business of managing his estate, but his wife is still full of vigor, "for she has not the anxieties, the travails, the cares he has..." (111). One of the writers in the Middle Ages who portrayed women with inordinate sexual desires was Jean de Meun. His jealous husband in *Le Roman de la Rose* violently condemns all women:

> "All you women are, will be, and have been whores, in fact or in
> desire, for, whoever could eliminate the deed, no man can constrain
> desire. All women have the advantage of being mistresses of their
> desires. For no amount of beating or upbraiding can change your
> hearts, but the man who could change you would have lordship
> over your bodies." (165-166)

Jean de Meun implies that there is not, and never will be, even one virtuous woman. Although the jealous husband speaks these words, and defenders of Jean de Meun protest that this character does not necessarily present the author's viewpoint, nothing elsewhere in de Meun's portion of *Le Roman de la Rose* suggests that virtue may be expected from women.

Several of Chaucer's tales also depict the lustful nature of women, although good naturedly rather than viciously. In "The Miller's Tale" and "The Merchant's Tale," for example, the situation is common—a young woman is married to an old man. She will naturally stray, but the foolish old man chasing youth is almost as much at fault as his straying wife. The Miller says of the carpenter who married young Alisoun, "He knew nat Catoun for his wit was rude,/ That bad man sholde wedde his simylitude./ Men sholde wedden after hire estaat,/ For youthe and elde is often at debaat" (ll. 3225-3230). Alisoun's young suitor Nicholas does not have to plead for very long before Alisoun promises to give him what he wants as soon as there is an opportunity. In "The Merchant's Tale," young May weds old Januarie, and soon attracts the attention of his squire Damyan. Damyan contrives to be alone with May and gives her a letter describing his passion. She manages to get some privacy in the privy when "She feyned hire as that she moste gon/ Ther as ye woot that every wight moot need" (ll. 1950-1951). There she memorizes the love letter and, tearing it to pieces, throws it down the privy (ll. 1952-1954). From that day on May thinks constantly of Damyon.

The speed with which the young wife's heart softens toward her lover reflects woman's malleable nature. Her cold moist humours will also make her deceitful and inventive (Maclean 42). Damyan has no trouble finding a way to seduce May. All he has to do is work on her volatile emotions and let nature take its course. He even depends on May's natural inventiveness to find a time for them to satisfy their desires—in a fruit tree in Januarie's private garden. Often in his work, Chaucer uses accepted stereotypes to tell good stories; whether or not he believes that all women are naturally lustful, the straying young wife provides him with a recognizable character who will provoke his audience to laughter. The fact that his are good stories and are read over and over again helps to perpetuate the stereotypes.

The concept of women as naturally lustful is also very common in the romances that were Sidney's literary models, from the Greek works by Heliodorus and Longus to such Renaissance texts as the *Amadis de Gaule* and Ariosto's *Orlando Furioso*. While Heliodorus's heroine Chariclea adventures through the entire romance fiercely protecting her chastity from pirates, her Egyptian captors, and even her true love Theagenes, the story has several examples of evil seductresses ruled by passion who plot against their husbands in order to satisfy their desires. One such is Dementa, the second wife of an old man, and the stepmother of young Cnemon (17-27). Dementa pretends to love Cnemon's father, but she really lusts after her stepson. Finally, one night when his father is away,

Dementa comes into Cnemon's bed. Naturally, young Cnemon withstands his stepmother. In anger, Dementa turns his father against him. She has her maid Thisbe seduce Cnemon (a fairly easy task, since Cnemon has been trying to seduce Thisbe for some time). Thisbe convinces Cnemon that his father is out of the house and that Dementa is lying with a lover. Cnemon rushes to their bedroom intending to kill Dementa and her lover, and discovers his father in bed with her. His father unnecessarily pleads with Cnemon for his life. Refusing to believe Cnemon's story, he ultimately banishes him from Athens. Thus, Dementa's lust has ruined Cnemon and destroyed a family. This story is repeated over and over in the history of literature; it is the story of Phaedre and Hippolytus and David and Potiphar's wife.[10] The fact that it survives in many Renaissance texts, however, testifies to a continued acceptance of the stereotype.

Although Heliodorus' heroine Chariclea is not lustful, she does demonstrate the weaknesses to be found in even the most virtuous female characters. Although she remains chaste throughout the story, she has a woman's "natural" deceitfulness, a characteristic usually associated with lustfulness. Whenever Theagenes and Chariclea are in a crisis that Theagenes' manly virtues of strength and courage cannot resolve, he turns to Chariclea for a devious plot that will save them. While Theagenes cannot invent the lies that come naturally to Chariclea, he is not above joining her in subterfuge. Directness is so foreign to Chariclea's nature that when her parents are about to sacrifice Theagenes to their gods, she can barely bring herself to tell the truth of his identity, which will save him. Since Chariclea does manage to maintain her chastity in the most trying and tempting situations, it seems obvious that Heliodorus intended her to be an example of the most virtuous of women; that she is also deceitful reflects the belief that women are, by nature, less virtuous than men.

Ariosto, too, describes the lust and deceitfulness of women. On one occasion, Rinaldo, Bradamante's brother, is offered a cup to test his wife's chastity; he declines, explaining,

> My wife a woman is, women are fraile,
> Yet, to believe the best I am enclinde;
> I know I cannot better my belief,
> And if I change it, it will by my grief. (Book XLIII, st. 9)

His host deems Rinaldo very wise, since no man who has ever used the cup has discovered that his wife is chaste. The host recounts the story about how he discovered his wife's dishonesty through the efforts of the enchantress Melyssa, usually a force for good in the romance. The host says that he had always kept his wife hidden away to insure himself of her chastity until Melyssa challenged him: "Your care, and not her vertue keeps her chaste" (XLIII, st. 25). For the test, Melyssa gave the host the shape of a young knight and changed herself into a page, and then they approached the host's wife with a jewelled casket containing pearls and other precious stones. The host pleaded and tempted until his wife agreed to what he wanted, at which point Melyssa changed his shape back again. His wife began to hate him, and finally slipped away with a young knight. The only thing he gained was the drinking cup, a gift from Melyssa to serve as consolation, since it proves that all wives are unchaste. Although Pamela Joseph Benson postulates that Ariosto is actually profeminist (101), it is interesting to note that he has a woman who is elevated above other women by her special powers deplore her own sex. This illustrates the common assumption that women without the tendency toward lust are supernatural, above their natures—like Melyssa herself.

To be fair to Ariosto, he also speaks of male weakness and often seems to find lust as much a masculine trait as a feminine one.[11] When Ruggiero finds Angelica staked out on a rock, naked, as prey for a monster, he fairly drools with lust as he sits down to stare at her body. He makes no attempt to free Angelica from her bonds until after the monster appears and has been vanquished. Then he throws her up on his flying horse and sets off to find a shady grove to enjoy the fruits of her gratitude. Unfortunately, he is in full armor and has a terrible time trying to get out of it:

> His armour made him yet a while to byde,
> Which forced stay, a more desire did breed,
> But now in him it was most truly tryde,
> Oftentimes the greater hast, the worse the speed,
> He knits with hast two knots, while one untyde. (X, st. 97)

This ridiculous picture of a knight frantically trying to take off his armor in order to fall on the girl becomes even more farcical when Angelica puts on a magic ring that makes her invisible. Ruggiero lunges around the grove like a blind man, trying to find Angelica with his hands. Finally he cries out,

> O cruell and unthankfull wench (he sayd),
> Dost thou reward him thus that brought thee ayd?
> To thy preserver art thou so unkind?
> Take ring, and shield, and flying horse and me,
> Only denie me not thy face to see.... (XI, st. 8)

Truly, it is not Angelica's face he wants to see! To give Ruggiero his due, all of this happens before he becomes a Christian, and in *Orlando Furioso* pagans are not expected to have the moral standards of Christians.

The reader must also realize that there is a flaw in Angelica herself. In the Renaissance, as well as in the Middle Ages, a man's lust for a particular woman usually was considered the fault of the woman. Courtesy books spend much time teaching women how to avoid attracting the attention of men; Vives would have women stay at home all the time "and not go abroad, except it be to hear divine service, and then well covered, lest they either give or take occasion of (en)snaring" (101). He admonishes women to keep their eyes lowered at all times, to remain silent, not to laugh when they are out, to walk at a measured pace—neither too slowly nor too fast—and to dress modestly (97). Violating any of these strictures will attract Ruggiero's kind of unwanted attention. Ariosto portrays Angelica as a wanton who attracts attention from men and causes them to fall from virtue. Because she has been inconstant in love, she may welcome attention from Ruggiero. First she loves Orlando, then Sacrapant, and finally, Cupid gets revenge for her inconstancy by causing her to love a lowly page, Medoro, on whom she forces herself (XIX, sts. 24-25). Even religious men cannot resist her lures; at one point, an old hermit looks at her, instantly lusts after her, and attempts to rape her. This echoes some of the teachings of the early church which describe women as the ultimate temptation to the holy state of chastity. St. John Chrysostom said, "How often do we, from beholding a woman, suffer a thousand evils: returning home, and entertaining an inordinate desire, and experiencing anguish for many days....The beauty of women is the greatest snare" (Bullough 98). Ariosto portrays the temptress Angelica with a lewd and ribald humor which is completely absent in his portrayal of Bradamante, whose chastity is never threatened, perhaps because she never swerves from her divinely ordained purpose—to find and marry Ruggiero. In her single-mindedness, Bradamante remains free of the most damning of all female vices, lust. Indeed, Ariosto portrays Bradamante with such solemnity that she is not at all as interesting as the livelier and much less virtuous Angelica.

Writers of the late Middle Ages and the early English Renaissance often depict the other greatly feared vice natural to women, domination of men, along with the garrulity and pride that accompany it. Jean de Meun strongly condemns women for the desire to dominate, claiming that it is born of malice. Once again, he accuses all women of this desire, and appears to believe that they will stop at nothing to satisfy it:

> No woman will ever be so ardent nor her love so secure that she may not wish to torment and despoil her sweetheart. But see what others do, who give themselves to men in return for gifts: one cannot find a single one of them who does not want to act in this way, so that she may have a man in subjection to her; they all have this intention. (153)

The speaker in this passage is not de Meun's Jealous Husband, whose words one would expect to be heated and exaggerated, but Friend. De Meun further asserts through his character Genius that a woman will tell secrets as soon as she learns them, and at the same time she will keep those secrets to use as a lever to control the marriage (276-277). He reveals men's fear of women, as well as fear of losing power.

The author of *The Fifteen Joys of Marriage* frequently discusses dominating wives. Like Jean de Meun, this author describes a woman's tongue as her major weapon in her fight to dominate her husband; in almost every chapter he speaks about the wife's scolding, wearing her husband down until he gives in to her. Pride is also at work, because the wife refuses to humble herself to her husband. Terrible things happen when a wife rules: children will be poorly taught, and unfit husbands will be chosen for the daughters (176-177). The whole family suffers, and in a broader sense, the ordered foundations of society are in danger because the husband who is submissive to his wife may not be submissive to his lord; he will not be able to serve two authorities.

Chaucer is not as concerned as the author of *The Fifteen Joys* with the dire effects of female domination on society as a whole. Once again, he seems more interested in storytelling than social commentary. His Wife of Bath delights in her domination of her first four husbands. From her point of view, most men are easy to manipulate, and that is enough reason for women to try. The only one of her husbands whom she could not dominate was Jankyn, with whom she achieved an alliance of equals. The Wife of Bath is a merry and thoroughly likeable woman; her garrulity seems jolly and pleasing to the modern reader, and probably did to the medieval reader also, but I wonder if the humor is not of the same variety that pokes fun at cuckolds: the situation is funny, provided that one is not married to that sort of woman—in this case, the woman who rules the roast through nagging and deceit. In this tale, Chaucer reflects the idea that women use their tongues to deceive, to divulge secrets, and to make men's lives miserable, but most of all, to dominate their husbands.

In the romances of the Middle Ages and the Renaissance, the dominating woman is often an enchantress seeking power over men for political reasons. In Malory's *Morte Darthur*, Morgan le Fay repeatedly tries to gain mastery over Arthur in order to depose him. She is so much Arthur's archenemy that much of the action revolves around her machinations. One of the ways she tries to win power is through the seduction Arthur's knights, most of whom nevertheless remain steadfast and loyal. Not lust but the desire for political power drives Morgan to these attempts at seduction. In one episode, having enchanted Sir Launcelot, she takes him to her castle where she tells him that even though he loves Guinevere, he must make love to her or one of her ladies or he will not be released. Similarly, in Ariosto's *Orlando Furioso*, Alcyna is an enchantress who lures honorable knights to her castle and bewitches them with the feminine delights of love. Ariosto vividly describes Alcyna's palace and her seduction of Ruggiero as so overwhelming and luxurious that he forgets both his prince and Bradamante, the lady he loves. However, none of this is Ruggiero's fault. Ariosto instructs us, "Ne must you blame Ruggiero's inclination,/ But rather blame the force of incantation" (VII, st. 17). Alcyna and Morgan le Fay manage to gain some sort of mastery over men only through magic, symbolic of women's power. Though women are by nature deceitful and desire dominance, virtuous men can withstand them unless the women use supernatural powers.

In some of Sidney's literary models, women gain mastery over men simply through the power of love, an unreasonable passion which makes men unnaturally subservient to women. In *Orlando Furioso*, when women control men (even through love), only bad things happen: Orlando goes mad when Angelica marries Medoro; Ruggiero forgets his duty when he is under the spell of Alcyna; a whole country suffers when Olympia insists on marrying her choice of suitor instead of her father's. Although there are no female characters in Sannazaro's *Arcadia*, the men constantly lament the force of love which puts them in their mistresses' power. They speak of women as cruel mistresses who cause suffering but do not suffer themselves. In Chapter Ten, Clonico performs a violent rite to make his mistress suffer as he does. He chants, while piercing a wax image of his beloved, cursing her and wishing her to suffer horrible affliction; to him, love is not a gentle or beautiful passion but a torment which generates both suffering and resentment (108). In Montemayor's *Diana*, one lady causes the deaths of a father and son because both love her and she cannot choose between them. Love, in these cases, is a force that reverses the natural order of things, making the lady superior to her lover, often provoking great tragedies.

Virtuous heroines, even the most independent of them, are never dominant in Sidney's models. Benson explains why in her discussion of *Orlando Furioso*:

> Despite the positive representation of women's capacities, their
> independence appears as a threat to society; autonomy can result
> in rebellion against marriage, reversed sexual hierarchies, and
> social chaos....The ideal accomplished woman submits to marriage,
> its hierarchy, and its limited field of activity. (172)

Although Benson is writing specifically about Ariosto's work, her comment applies generally as well. In *Orlando Furioso*, although Ruggiero treats Bradamante with courtesy (when he is in her presence—otherwise, he is likely to forget her), he is never her slave; that would be inappropriate, since he is going to marry her. Indeed, Bradamante is herself a model of obedience. Since she is not yet married to Ruggiero, she must obey her father. When he commands her to marry the heir of the Emperor of Greece instead of Ruggiero, Bradamante stands silent and torn, feeling obligated to honor her promise to Ruggiero yet unwilling to disobey her parents. Thus the warrior maid who has competed against men in trials of arms and who has made many moral decisions in her travels stands submissive to a command she knows to be wrong; Melyssa has previously revealed to her that she and Ruggiero will found a great line. Like Griselda, Bradamante is completely willing to leave her future in the hands of the men she has been taught to obey.

The female characters in the works of Sidney's literary predecessors are static, either good or evil. In fact, they don't change at all; usually only male characters like Ruggiero change.[12] For the most part, female characters are recognizable stereotypes whose behavior is easily predictable. Sidney alters the pattern of women who are either passive and virtuous or active and evil in his creation of women who do not fit the stereotypes. His villainesses do not have supernatural powers, but they do have superior intelligence, and they are not necessarily completely evil. Further, Sidney deviates from his predecessors in that he allows his major female characters to grow and change; they experience the temptations of love and become strong enough to withstand them. Finally, his heroines do not quietly wait for the heroes to save them from evil situations; they rather demonstrate moral courage when they resist and even attack their wicked captors. As Sidney's work progressed from 1580 when he finished the *Old Arcadia* to 1583 when he suspended his work on the *New Arcadia*, his female characters differ increasingly from the women in his models: they become less stereotypical and more individual.

NOTES

1 I have also used extensively Diane Bornstein's study of medieval courtesy literature, *The Lady in the Tower* and Ruth Kelso's *Doctrine for the Lady of the Renaissance*, which is a broadly based study of Renaissance courtesy literature.

2 Aristotle and Galen both postulated that "woman is less fully developed than man. Because of lack of heat in generation, her sexual organs have remained internal..." (Maclean 31). Thus, the uterus is an inverted penis, and the ovaries are internal testes. For a discussion of the various theories about female physiology see Maclean, pages 28–46.

3 Vives further adds that these books must be read with the proper attitude; if parents fear that their daughters are reading "with an ill will and loath thereto," they should be denied all further access to education (62).

4 In fact, "Frequent sexual intercourse, according to medical opinion, was necessary for female health, for without it the uterus might dry up" (Brundage 376). In her article on Vives in *Silent but for the Word* (Ed. Margaret Patterson Hannay), Vallerie Wayne states:

> All of Vives' restrictions on the lives of women are given in the name of chastity, and the virtue was lauded and praised so much during the Renaissance that it obscured the other virtues a woman might exhibit or strive for. One good for women had become the only good.
>
> (24)

5 See Stone, *Family, Sex and Marriage* p. 217 on flogging as accepted punishment for wives, children, and miscreants in the 16th and 17th centuries.

6 Christine was greatly incensed by Jean de Meun's assertion in *Le Roman de la Rose* that all women desire to gain mastery over their husbands and lovers by discovering and spreading their secrets. She says, referring to de Meun and others,

> I pray all those who truly hold this teaching authentic and put so much faith in it, that they kindly tell me how many men they have seen accused, killed, hanged, and publicly rebuked by accusations of their women? (Baird 51)

7 Betty S. Travitsky notes in *The Renaissance English Women in Print: Counterbalancing the Canon* that "while humanist and Protestant theorists paid startlingly new attention to women's minds, they did so to uplift women's personal spirituality and to equip them better for their traditional, domestic roles. Moreover, the theorists plied their attentions unevenly. The humanists simply did not develop a practical system for educating women, and the only women affected by their relatively esoteric theories were therefore noblewomen and (occasionally) women from humanist or court-affiliated families of lower status, like the Mores and Cookes" (24).

8 The courtesy books do not address the question of a female ruler; although Vives wrote specifically for the instruction of Mary Tudor, he did not expect her to rule in her own right. He teaches her to obey her husband, just as any wife should.

9 Theories of courtly love actually stressed that this kind of romantic love could only exist outside of marriage (Terry ix).

10 Cyril Tourneur used this story in *The Revenger's Tragedy*, which appeared in 1607.

11 Benson claims that "Ariosto demonstrates that man's problem with woman arises from his own limitations, from considering her an earthly good and object of desire whose steadfastness can be maintained by material restraints rather than by considering her as an independent being to be wooed and loved and won through steadfast faith and unselfish love" (121).

12 Generally, the only women who repent and change are found in saints' legends and Scripture, when they go from one extreme to the other. Sidney manages to avoid the extremes; although she repents and changes, Gynecia does not become a saint.

The *Old Arcadia*

Sidney's first full-length fiction was his *Old Arcadia*, probably begun at Wilton in 1580 (Robertson xvi). In this work he created three major female characters: the heroines Pamela and Philoclea and their mother Gynecia. Sidney uses stereotypes to form his female characters more extensively here than he does in any of his subsequent works, but even in this early endeavor he does not simply perpetuate the stereotypes. Pamela and Philoclea are, rather, collections of various stereotypes. Sometimes the princesses seem to be completely virtuous romance heroines, but at other times they exhibit the frailties that writers of conduct manuals considered natural to women. However, they are never more than silhouettes, pursued and wooed in the accepted romance manner, and their main function in the plot is to provide Pyrocles and Musidorus with love objects, obstacles in the path of heroic endeavor which cause the heroes to become hopelessly inactive and even effeminate.

Sidney leaves stereotypes behind in his creation of Gynecia, the mother of the princesses. Unlike Pamela and Philoclea, she is a strongly individual character, actively influencing the events of the story, yet, unlike the strong female characters of Sidney's predecessors, she is not evil. Gynecia is a forceful, intelligent woman, capable of moral reasoning, who succumbs to her guilty passion for Pyrocles and becomes willing to commit adultery and to sacrifice her daughter to achieve her desire. However, Sidney allows her to repent, to recover from the disease of passion, and to retain her high station and her reputation for virtue. She is the only character who learns from experience and who changes. Sidney's predecessors allowed only male characters like Lancelot and Ruggiero to sin, repent, and change. Female characters seldom cross the line from sinner to saint; Alcyna and Morgan le Fay do not consider the good or evil of their conduct because evil is all they know. Gynecia, on the other hand, is always aware of her sin and spends much time reviling herself for her illicit passion. Villainesses of Sidney's predecessors do not exhibit such psychological complexity. Thus, Sidney diverges from literary and cultural stereotypes in his creation of a woman who is not simply good or evil, but a complex mixture of the two. Two other considerations influenced Sidney's handling of major female characters in the *Old Arcadia*: his designated audience and the role of his narrator. Sidney wrote the *Old Arcadia* specifically for women and especially for his sister Mary, the Countess of Pembroke. In his dedicatory letter, he describes himself as "the writer who doth exceedingly love [her]..." (*OA* 3). As the story progresses, he often addresses his sister and her friends in asides as "fair ladies."[1] Sidney's descriptions of Pamela and Philoclea often seem to be tongue-in-cheek, whereas he seems to be much more serious when he describes Gynecia.

Since authors like Lyly were beginning to write romances specifically for women (Hull 8), Sidney may have been calling attention to female characterization in this genre, and he may well have been teasing his sister about the kind of stories women were believed to prefer. Certainly the nature of women probably was not his primary concern, as it probably was not the major concern of his intelligent and well-read audience.[2] The fact that in the *Old Arcadia* Sidney addresses such serious issues as politics and philosophy demonstrates his respect for his female audience. I believe that he expected them to understand that he created Pamela and Philoclea from clichés in order to emphasize that that is exactly what they were, and that, just as deliberately, he created Gynecia on a different plane as a serious and complex study in human nature. Sidney's narrator does not merely tell the story. He often speaks directly to the readers, guiding the audience's responses to the actions of the characters. Sometimes these comments are harsh and judgmental, but usually the direct address precedes one of the teasing comments about the nature of women which lighten the tone of the book and make the reader wonder if she should take the narrator's moralizing completely seriously. Elizabeth Dipple apparently understands the narrator's observations to be Sidney's commentary to his designated audience. She states that "Whenever Sidney's voice intrudes into the text...the reader must make a decision about the nature of the authorial interruption. The very diversity of voices...forces a pause in the narrative flow while the decision is being made, an aspect of audience participation that would be perfectly natural to Sidney as he handed each completed sheet...to his sister" ("Unjust Justice" 85). Richard Lanham, on the other hand, perceives a narrative voice that is sometimes, but not always, Sidney's. Lanham notes that "it is a mistake to make out a complete distinction between the 'real' Sidney and 'Sidney the narrator', for the distance between them frequently changes" (321). He adds, "Sidney's tongue is more fully in his cheek at some times than at others" (322), and he says that Sidney depended on his small intimate audience to understand him—some things just did not have to be explained (329). I believe that the narrator's voice is always Sidney's, but his attitudes vary as he writes, just as in conversation with friends one may sometimes toss out a jibe meant to elicit a groan acknowledging a hit, and at other times one may be completely engrossed in the seriousness of the topic. The narrator's changing tone is an indication of Sidney's close and affectionate relationship with his audience; as Mary Ellen Lamb states, "His teasing tone suggests the intimacy born of prolonged association, through which he has learned their [his reader's] foibles but does not judge them" (77). However, these shifts in tone make it difficult for the modern reader to interpret Sidney's intent in every situation, but an awareness of his relationship to his audience and an understanding of Elizabethan attitudes toward women can guide us in our interpretations of his female characters in the *Old Arcadia*.

I

The action of the *Old Arcadia* begins when Basilius, the Duke of Arcadia, consults an oracle which advises him that:

> Thy elder care shall from thy careful face
> By princely mean be stolen and yet not lost;
> Thy younger shall with nature's bliss embrace
> An uncouth love, which nature hateth most.
> Thou with thy wife adult'ry shalt commit,
> And in thy throne a foreign state shall sit.
> All this on thee this fatal year shall hit. (5)

In order to avoid his enigmatically stated fate and despite wise counsel from his chief advisor Philanax, Basilius decides to go into retirement in the Arcadian countryside, virtually abdicating.   To forestall the predictions concerning his daughters, Basilius isolates them. Pamela, his heir, he puts into the keeping of the rustic buffoon Dametas, his wife Miso, and his daughter Mopsa. His younger daughter, Philoclea, is to be secluded in another dwelling with himself and her mother Gynecia. No well-born men will be allowed to approach either. However, he reckons without the ingenuity of Pyrocles and Musidorus, princes and cousins who are travelling through Asia Minor and Greece doing heroic deeds on their way to Pyrocles' homeland. When Pyrocles falls in love with Philoclea's portrait, he disguises himself as an Amazon, Cleophila, in order to approach the court; then Musidorus disguises himself as a shepherd, Dorus, when he catches a glimpse of Pamela and falls in love with her. The princes abandon heroics and concentrate on satisfying their desires. To add to the confusion, Gynecia quickly penetrates Pyrocles' disguise and falls in love with him, while Basilius falls in love with Cleophila the Amazon. The rest of the story revolves around the princes' efforts to gain the princesses' love and to consummate that love.

Sidney occasionally presents Pamela and Philoclea through their own thoughts and words, but more often through descriptions of them and epithets attached to their names by the narrator and other characters. Especially revealing are the attitudes of Pyrocles and Musidorus, who reflect in their conversations the Elizabethan assumption of the inferiority of women. The princes demonstrate again and again that they regard the princesses as objects of gratification rather than as women with feelings of their own. The princesses themselves speak very little to anyone except Pyrocles and Musidorus. In fact, their most consistent characteristic is silence, and Sidney's narrator often reports and summarizes their few speeches. They are thus isolated from each other and from all of the other characters but their lovers. At the outset Pamela and Philoclea are passive, meek, and silent heroines whose virtue has never been tested until they meet Pyrocles and Musidorus. After Sidney establishes this outline, he moves from stereotype to clichés concerning the frailty of women found in such courtesy handbooks as *The Book of the Knight of the Tower*. Pyrocles and Musidorus easily persuade the malleable Pamela and Philoclea to actions counter to all ideas of virtue: Pamela's pride leads her to agree to an illegal elopement with Musidorus in opposition to her father's vehement wishes, and Philoclea falls from the very pinnacle of female virtue in losing her virginity to Pyrocles—actions quite atypical of traditional romance heroines. However, Sidney maintains the reader's sympathy for the heroines by emphasizing their youth, their beauty, the strength of their passion, and the even more guilty behavior of their lovers and their parents, Basilius and Gynecia.

Sidney quickly sketches the outlines of Pamela and Philoclea. Philoclea is the ideal heroine—beautiful, sweet, chaste; Pamela is less beautiful but modestly dignified and accomplished. From then on, he has but to use an epithet such as "the gracious Pamela" (101) or "the sweet Philoclea" (123) to bring these characters into focus; their attributes explain both their strengths and weaknesses. Philoclea's humility and innocence, desirable traits in a well-protected woman, would make her impressionable and susceptible to temptations of love. Pamela's dignity and majesty might mean that she is too proud to be properly obedient. Sidney himself subtly reminds his audience of the common belief in women's inferiority when he describes the sisters as

> both so excellent in all those gifts which are allotted to reasonable creatures as they seemed to be born for a sufficient proof that nature is no stepmother to that sex how much soever the rugged disposition of some men, sharp-witted only in evil speaking, hath sought to disgrace them. (4-5)

In disclaiming the negative theories about women, Sidney actually focuses the reader's attention on them, and since he writes for his sister and her friends, I suspect that this is one of the passages designed to gently tease. Sidney makes several references to the understood weaknesses of women so that his audience is not surprised when the heroines slip from their pedestals into the waiting arms of their lovers.

The first mention of Philoclea in Book I emphasizes her beauty. Stereotypically, beauty in a woman may be either good or evil: on the one hand, outer beauty reflects inner beauty; on the other, a beautiful woman cannot be a good woman since she has so many opportunities to fall. In his initial description of Philoclea, Sidney concentrates on her innocence, but as the story progresses, he manages to incorporate both concepts of the nature of beautiful women into the princess whom the narrator calls "the beauty of the world" (9). She is so lovely that Pyrocles has only to see her portrait to fall in love with her long before he ever meets her. Philoclea's portrait reveals her innocence: "therein, besides the show of her beauties, a man might judge even the nature of her countenance, full of bashfulness, love, and reverence—and all by the cast of her eye—, mixed with a sweet grief to find her virtue suspected" (11). Obviously, Philoclea is the perfect Elizabethan female: loving, chaste, and sweetly submissive (as indicated by her bashfulness and reverence). Her beauty is enough to change a young hero into a passionate lover.

Sidney reveals the princes' ideas about love and the women who inspire it when Musidorus discovers with horror that Pyrocles intends to disguise himself as an Amazon in order to be near Philoclea. Sidney puts in Musidorus' mouth the arguments against women current in Elizabethan society, while Pyrocles voices Elizabethan arguments in favor of women to justify his passion and his actions. Sidney uses this dialectic to focus his female audience's attention on the conventional ideas about women. Musidorus finally declares that "this effeminate love of a woman doth so womanize a man that, if you yield to it, it will not only make you a famous Amazon, but a launder, a distaff-spinner, or whatsoever other vile occupation their idle heads can imagine and their weak hands perform" (20). Any unmanly weakness, especially love, is "effeminate." Musidorus himself, however, speaks only from dry rational theory, not from experience. As soon as he sees Pamela, all of his logic evaporates, and he falls as hard as his friend; the reader cannot take the arguments of either of these young men seriously, since both allow passion to rule them, and, although both speak as if they are Neoplatonic lovers led by earthly beauty to contemplate divine beauty, what they most ardently pursue is physical satisfaction.

In the course of his philosophical argument in favor of love, Pyrocles reveals that he really regards his beloved as an object of gratification. Beginning his justification on a lofty plane, he claims that women are worthy of love because "they are capable of virtue." He adds to clinch the argument, "And virtue, you yourself say, is to be loved..." (21). But he goes on to indicate that he is not really interested in Philoclea's virtue; that argument merely demonstrates to

Musidorus that Pyrocles knows the proper formula to justify love. What draws Pyrocles to Philoclea is her beauty: "But this I willingly confess: that it likes me much better when I find virtue in a fair lodging than when I am bound to seek it in an ill-favored creature, like a pearl in a dunghill" (21). With these words, Pyrocles' language descends from that of the high-minded Neoplatonic philosopher to that of any ordinary young man who has seen a pretty face. He reassures Musidorus that, even though he is wearing woman's clothing, he is still all man: "Neither doubt you, because I wear woman's apparel, I will be the more womanish; since, I assure you, for all my apparel, there is nothing more I desire than to fully prove myself a man in this enterprise" (22-23). He has no thought of marriage; his sole aim in this "enterprise," he tells Musidorus, is "Enjoying" (23) the object of his passion, and Philoclea's virtue doesn't really enter into his plans (except as it gets in the way of his "Enjoying"). The fact that Pyrocles proclaims his manhood in his feminine attire undercuts both his heroic nature and the value of his illicit love, and demonstrates that Sidney is laughing at this over-heated young man. When "womanish" passion strikes Pyrocles, he dons women's clothes, loses his virtuous masculine reason, and responds quickly, unthinkingly, and physically, just as medieval and Renaissance society expected (naturally lustful) women to respond.

Renaissance courtesy books reflect the idea that women somehow provoke lustful attention; therefore, the authors of these books spend much time exhorting women to stay home, to keep eyes downcast if they must go out, and to dress simply and modestly. When Sidney finally brings Philoclea on stage, he describes her apparel in such a way as to indicate that she unwittingly invites passion:

> The ornament of the earth, young Philoclea, appeared in her nymphlike apparel, so near nakedness as one might well discern part of her perfections, and yet so apparelled as did show she kept the best store of her beauties to herself...her body covered with a light taffeta garment, so cut as the wrought smock came through it in many places (enough to have made a restrained imagination have thought what was under it); with the sweet cast of her black eye which seemed to make a contention whether that in perfect blackness or her skin in perfect whiteness, were the most excellent;

> then, I say, the very clouds seemed to give place to make the
> heaven more fair. (37)

If Pyrocles' Amazonian garb reflects his fall from reason to womanish passion, then Philoclea's obviously seductive clothing might well reflect a certain natural but still innocent female sexuality (Weiner 95). What were her parents thinking of to allow her to appear before even rude shepherds in such dress—or undress? Sidney's Elizabethan readers would expect Philoclea's chastity to be in danger. Only her youth, innocence, and isolation could allow readers to believe in her virtue when they read this passage. Like Ariosto's Angelica, who invites male attention, Philoclea is not without blame when Pyrocles pursues her. However, since Philoclea is still under the supervision of her parents, whose folly is even more serious, she is not entirely at fault.

Sidney introduces Pamela in the same scene in which he shows us Philoclea, emphasizing different stereotypes in his juxtaposition of them. In Pamela, Sidney demonstrates nobility of character and dignity of bearing under trying circumstances—the female virtue of silent longsuffering advocated by The Knight of the Tower and Christine de Pisan. The narrator describes her as "The fair Pamela, whose noble heart had long disdained to find the trust of her virtue reposed in the hands of a shepherd..." (36). Her clothing, rather than being nymphlike, is the rough garb of the shepherds, donned "to show an obedience [to her father]..." (37). But again, there is another side to an apparent virtue. Pamela dresses as her parents wish in order "to *show* an obedience"—not in true obedience to her father's desire. Is the obedience itself merely show? In a discussion of the emblem Pamela wears on a chain around her neck, a lamb chained to a stake, Weiner notes the discrepancies between Pamela's outward appearance and her inner feelings:

> Pamela, though she makes a show of obedience to her father's
> commands, mocks them in the *impresa* she designed and wears, "a
> perfect white lamb tied at a stake with a great number of chains,
> as it had been feared lest the silly creature should do some great
> harm." (37)

He adds later,

Given the great stress on the duty and reverence owed to parents
by the Elizabethans, Pamela's disdain, even before it becomes
outright rebellion, is...[a] reminder of the unpleasant gap between
what ought to be and what is. (95)

The important clue to Pamela's character is that there *is* a gap between "what is"
and "what ought to be." Outwardly, she submits to her father, but her heart is
rebellious; there is a crack in Pamela's virtue. Although he raises no question of
her chastity, Sidney shows the reader that she is not well versed in that other
important Elizabethan female virtue, submission.

Sidney reaffirms the stereotypes he has already used to create the princesses
and re-emphasizes the princes' attitudes toward them as Pamela and Philoclea flee
from wild beasts, a lion and a bear, which suddenly invade the countryside where
the Arcadians have come to hear the shepherd-poets' eclogues. Pyrocles is aware
of Philoclea's beauty as the lion chases her: her "light nymphlike apparel...[is]
carried up with the wind, that much of those beauties she would at another time
have willingly hidden were presented to the eye" (47). His passions ignited, he so
enjoys Philoclea's beauties that he does not "follow her over hastily lest...[he]
should too soon deprive...[himself] of...pleasure" (47-48). Despite the Neoplatonic
platitudes he offered to Musidorus, Pyrocles loves Philoclea mainly for her beauty.
Indeed, the highest forms of secular love—Neoplatonic or courtly—would require
Pyrocles to put the comfort and well-being of his beloved above his own; instead,
he prolongs Philoclea's terror so that he can enjoy looking at her usually hidden
beauties longer.

When Musidorus defends his princess from the bear, his love is revealed to
be as guilty as Pyrocles'. By this time, Musidorus, who spoke so eloquently
against women, has confessed his love for Pamela to Pyrocles and has assumed his
disguise as a shepherd. While Pyrocles assumes another sex in his disguise,
Musidorus assumes another station. Each prince ironically and unwittingly chooses
the disguise most calculated to discomfort his beloved—Pyrocles' femininity
confounds Philoclea's latent sexuality, and Musidorus' lowliness offends Pamela's
stately pride. When she sees the bear coming towards her, Pamela faints, and
Musidorus jumps before her to kill the bear. Then he embraces her in a hug only
a little less distasteful to the proud princess than the bear's would have been:

"...softly taking her in his arms, he took the advantage to kiss and re-kiss her a hundred times, with such exceeding delight that he would often after say he thought the joy would have carried his life from him, had not the grief he conceived to see her in such case something diminished it" (52). Like Pyrocles, Musidorus takes advantage of his beloved when she cannot help herself—the grief that caused Pamela to faint only "something diminished" Musidorus' joy in his possession of her body. In fact, Musidorus seems to find Pamela most tempting when she is unconscious; perhaps the dignified princess awake is simply too dominating to excite Musidorus. When she comes to herself, Pamela "with great disdain put him from her" (52). Her action as well as the manner of it ("with great disdain") demonstrates her pride and her awareness of her position as Basilius' heir (and the lowly status of the shepherd), while Musidorus' actions demonstrate that he, like Pyrocles, regards his beloved as an object of gratification.

In Book I Sidney has portrayed the virtues of Pamela and Philoclea, but he has also foreshadowed their failures. In Book II he demonstrates that Philoclea's sweet and humble nature leads her to her downfall as she exchanges lawful obedience to her father for guilty submission to her lover. Sidney uses conventional terms to describe Philoclea's descent into what the princess believes to be a shameful passion: "She found a burning affection towards Cleophila; an unquiet desire to be with her; and yet she found that the very presence kindled desire" (98). Yet she does not struggle to overcome her apparently homosexual passion; instead, she resigns herself to it:

> Sometimes she would wish Cleophila had been a man, and her brother; and yet, in truth, it was no brotherly love she desired of her. But then, like a sweet mind not much traversed in the cumbers of these griefs, she would even yield to the burden, rather suffering the sorrow to take a full possession than exercising any way her mind how to redress it. (97-98)

Sidney demonstrates how Philoclea's innocence and sweetness, usually admirable qualities in a young girl, make her vulnerable to passion, especially since her parents are too intensely pursuing their own desires to pay attention to their daughter. Philoclea is young, and her virtue is untried. Her parents' removal to

Arcadia has released her from all emotional restraints and has left her without the guides and protectors society believed a female needs to keep her virtuous. She is ready to fall.

The stereotypical frailty that Sidney brings out in Philoclea is her malleability. As soon as Pyrocles discovers her passion, he begins to use her nature for his own ends—"enjoying," as he told Musidorus. When he reveals his true identity to her, he insists, "My suit is to serve you, and my end to do you honour" (120). Like Chaucer's Damyon, he says only what he thinks will win his beloved; he has forgotten all about honor as long as passion rules. And Philoclea, instead of leaving Pyrocles once she knows he is a man, softened by her own passion and Pyrocles' words, stays to hear what he has to say. Soon, she begins to pity Pyrocles, and her humility leads her to accept all the guilt for his passion, as she echoes the cliché which blames women and exonerates men in cases of sexual misconduct. This is a recurring theme in Philoclea's speech; whenever there is misunderstanding or tension in her relationship with Pyrocles, she is quick to believe that it is her fault. At times, Sidney makes Philoclea a drooping caricature of maidenly submission, as when she says, "If I had continued as I ought Philoclea, you had either never been or ever been Cleophila....But I fear me my behavior ill governed gave you...[encouragement]" (212). She soon moves from accepting all blame to complete surrender, comparing herself with a castle besieged and won:

> If my castle had seemed weak, you would never have brought these disguised forces. No, no; I have betrayed myself. It was well seen I was glad to yield before I was assaulted....Thou has then the victory; use it now with virtue, since from the steps of virtue my soul is witness to itself it never hath, and pledge to itself it never shall decline no way to make me leave to love thee, but by making me think thy love unworthy of me. (121-122)

Philoclea's maidenly submissiveness has opened her to Pyrocles' manipulation. Having detached her from her parental loyalty, he has molded her to his own design. She offers Pyrocles the submission that rightfully still belongs to her parents, and knowing she is in his power, begs him to treat her virtuously.

In parallel scenes, Sidney demonstrates that the proud Pamela is also stereotypically malleable as she, like Philoclea, guiltily submits to her lover. At first, Pamela resists her growing passion for one she believes to be a lowly shepherd. Like Philoclea, she has had strange feelings growing in her:

> For indeed Pamela, having had no small stirring of her mind
> towards him [Musidorus], as well for the goodliness of his shape
> as for the excellent trial of his courage, had notwithstanding, with
> a true-tempered virtue, sought all this while to overcome it; and a
> great mastery, although not without pain, she had wrought with
> herself. (98)

Pamela apparently has the fortitude necessary to overcome her passion; however, her virtue is inspired, at least in part, by her dignity—her recognition of her station makes the love of a shepherd just as impossible to Pamela as love of a woman is to Philoclea. Pamela's dignity is a virtue as long as it motivates her to accept with graciousness all of the discomforts of her position as Dametas' ward; it becomes a feminine frailty when it leads her to rebellion.

Pamela's pride becomes a vice when Musidorus pretends to court Mopsa in order to approach his true object. She begins "to have the more consideration of him....For indeed so falls it often in the excellent women that even that which they disdain to themselves yet like they not that others should will it from them" (99). The ironic teasing of the comment emphasizes Pamela's feminine desire to remain in control of the situation. Her jealousy pricks her to question Musidorus, ostensibly on behalf of the bewildered Mopsa, and she soon realizes that the shepherd is not what he seems. In the course of her examination she exchanges flirtatious banter with him. This badinage does not appear to be of any great importance until one remembers that Pamela is the heir to her father's country, and has even greater responsibility than other women to keep herself pure. If her dignity were truly virtuous, it would make her always aware of her duty; when she flirts with a shepherd, her pride appears to be founded on self-regard.

As Musidorus tells the story of his royal background, Pamela retreats into silence, as though she could spar with him while he seems to be a lowly shepherd but must be demure when he becomes an eligible suitor. For example, when

Musidorus pauses in the story and waits for a permission to continue, Pamela says nothing, only "showing by her countenance that [his continued conversation] was her pleasure..." (104). Pamela is changing her mind about Musidorus—she accepts him as a superior male; in Castiglione's *The Courtier*, the women respond to the men in their circle in much the same way, indicating by nods and smiles that they approve of what the men say. When Peter Bembo suggests a discussion of "which is the greater grief, eyther to dysplease the wight beloved, or to recyve dyspleasure of the wyght beloved," Lady Emilia responds silently: "without anye woord spekyng to Bembo, she tourned her head and made a signe to Sir Frederick Fegoso to shew hes devyse" (41). Although the situations are different, the response to male conversation is the same. Like the ladies in *The Courtier*, Pamela maintains her virtuous silence once Musidorus convinces her of his station. Like Pyrocles, Musidorus uses his beloved's feminine weaknesses to mold her to his will. He soon persuades her to flee with him for these reasons: "the virtuous gratefulness for his affection; then, knowing him to be a prince; and lastly, seeing herself in unworthy bondage" (107). Musidorus appeals to Pamela's misplaced self-esteem and her rebelliousness to gain her confidence.

In Musidorus' conversation with Pamela, Sidney plays with the ideas that women are naturally proud and desire to have their own way. To make clear how far Pamela deviates from virtuous behavior, he ironically gives conventional words of feminine virtue to lowly Mopsa, who thinks that Dorus the shepherd has been wooing her. She exclaims that "for all his quaint speeches, she would keep her honesty close enough. And that, as for the high way of matrimony, she would go never a furlong further till my master, her father, did speak the whole word himself" (108). Sound advice for an Elizabethan maiden who belonged to her father and owed him complete obedience! However, once her pride gains the upper hand, Pamela will listen to the lowly Mopsa no more than she would marry a lowly shepherd, and she, like Philoclea, yields to her lover.

Once the princes have won the submission of their mistresses, they immediately plot their final goal: enjoying. Musidorus sends Dametas and his family off on wild goose chases to get them out of his way, and Pyrocles convinces Basilius, who has had second thoughts about his voluntary exile, to stay in Arcadia. Musidorus plans to ride away with Pamela and to invade Arcadia with an army, if necessary, to force Basilius' consent to the marriage of Pyrocles and Philoclea. As she leaves with Musidorus, Pamela realizes that she has put herself in her lover's power. Like Philoclea, she asks her lover to use her virtuously:

> Let me be your own (as I am), but by no unjust conquest. Let not our joys, which ought ever to last, be stained in our own conscien- ces.... I have yielded to be your wife; stay then till the time that I may rightly be so.... What should I more say? If I have chosen well, all doubt is past, since your action only must determine whe- ther I have done virtuously or shamefully in following you. (196-197)

While Philoclea's request for Pyrocles to act virtuously is a cry of helplessness, Pamela's request for virtuous action from Musidorus is a reasoned argument, an unemotional laying out of facts, although events demonstrate that she is just as helpless as her sister in the presence of her lover's passion. Sidney's portrayal of Pamela reflects Elizabethan ideas that women are not rational creatures; ironically, Pamela has carefully and proudly considered her options, and, woman-like, has reasoned incorrectly, choosing to break the law by riding away with Musidorus rather than suffer any more damage to her self-esteem.

Perhaps Musidorus rides off with Pamela intending to guard her virtue as she has asked him to, but as soon as she falls asleep, passion overcomes the prince and he tries to rape her. The double standard begins to operate. Pamela does nothing to provoke Musidorus' attack beyond placing herself in his power; lust does not overtake Musidorus until Pamela is asleep. Then, he bends "to take the advantage of the weakness of the watch, and see whether at that season he could win the bulwark" (202). The "bulwark" he intends to win is Pamela's virginity. As in Book I when he kisses the unconscious princess after protecting her from the bear, he is tempted to attack only when his lady is helpless and vulnerable to attack. His behavior is even more reprehensible because Pamela has placed herself in his care and proven her trust by peacefully falling asleep. He hopes to accomplish his aim "before timely help might come" (202), yet he, the one who has pledged to "help" Pamela, plans to degrade her further than her father and Dametas ever did. His desire to "help" Pamela is really a desire to get her alone so that he can "enjoy" her, for to him she is only an object of pleasure. Ironically, Pamela is saved from Musidorus' lawless passion by a band of outlawed Phagonian rebels, "to the just punishment of his broken promise, and most infortunate bar of his long-pursued and almost-achieved desires" (202).

In the meantime, as Musidorus plots to get rid of Dametas and his family in order to steal away with Pamela, Pyrocles single-mindedly pursues unlawful physical consummation with Philoclea. He manages to convince both Gynecia and Basilius that he finds them desirable and makes them both think they will meet him in a nearby cave, thus clearing the field for his attack on Philoclea's chastity. In order to convince Gynecia that he shares her passion, he focuses all of his attention on her while deliberately slighting Philoclea, even though he knows that his seeming change of heart is crushing Philoclea's tender nature. He is too concerned about obtaining his own physical desires, however, to worry about the pain he causes his beloved.

Pyrocles moves into action as soon as he has tricked Gynecia and Basilius into leaving the house. He locks all of the doors (he thinks), and heads for Philoclea's bedchamber. Philoclea, convinced that Pyrocles prefers her mother, lies in her bed "with a kindly meekness taking upon herself the weight of her own woes, and suffering them to have so full a course in her as it did not a little weaken the state of her body" (216). As he enters her room, he sees her "upon the top of her bed, having her beauties eclipsed with nothing but with a fair smock..." (231), in tears, lamenting her lost love. When Philoclea sees Pyrocles, she does not virtuously send him away; rather she takes him to task for his lack of faithfulness. However, her gentle nature will not long allow Philoclea to chastise her lover, although she resists Pyrocles' passionate declarations, even when he offers proof that he loves her and not her mother. He explains, "I have rid them both out of the house. There is none here to be either hinderers or knowers of the perfecting the mutual love which once my love wrought in you towards me..." (234).

All of Pyrocles' plots have been aimed at this moment. He is determined to gratify his desire, and nothing that Philoclea says or does will stop him. Pyrocles sets about enjoying in earnest, "using the benefit of time, and fortifying himself with the confessing her late fault (to make her now the sooner yield to penance), turning the passed griefs and unkindness to the excess of all kind joys...beginning now to envy Argus's thousand eyes, and Briareus's hundred hands..." (243). He turns Philoclea's soft impressionable nature against her, making her feel guilty for falsely accusing him in order to get past any residual sense of virtue she may have. His own pleasure is all he thinks of. Worse, he does not stop with words; he fights "against a weak resistance, which did strive to be overcome..." (243). Because Philoclea makes only a token resistance she illustrates, perhaps ironically, the accepted belief that women enjoy, even invite, rape. In 1405 Christine de Pisan deplored this notion about women: "I am...troubled and grieved when men argue that many women want to be raped and that it does not bother them at all to be raped by men even when they verbally protest" (161). Philoclea reacts the way Christine says that men think women react to rape; once Pyrocles masters her, it seems that Philoclea settles down to enjoy the experience. In this way, Sidney once again uses accepted Renaissance ideas about women to sketch his heroine; like Angelica, Philoclea invites seduction (or worse) with her beauty and her suggestive clothes. However, he also portrays her as young, innocent, and unaware of the effect she has on Pyrocles, whose only goal is "enjoying."[3] The reader might be tempted to see this passage as a romantic triumph of young love; however, Sidney has taken great pains to describe the disastrous effects passion has had on Pyrocles, as well as the rest of his characters. To view this scene as anything but a sinful travesty of virtue would require the reader to forget all that has come before it.

Sidney exonerates Pamela and Philoclea for their failures of virtue by isolating them from their natural guides, their parents. Throughout the story the princesses have had no one to confide in except their lovers; for the most part, they remain wrapped in silence. Until they are locked into the same room in the captivity scene at the end of the story, they never speak to each other even when they are together on the occasions of the shepherds' eclogues, so that in Book V the princesses still do not know the state of each other's emotions. In Book I, after Pamela and Philoclea have been rescued by Pyrocles and Musidorus, they begin to feel something hitherto unknown to them, and they hide these strange new feelings from each other. In the second eclogues, Histor recounts the heroic exploits of Pyrocles and Musidorus, who have revealed their true identities to their mistresses. The sisters, sitting side by side, are so engrossed in their own feelings that they do not notice each other's reactions: "either's heart was so plunged in her own that she never pained herself to call in question her sister's case; so that neither Pamela ever took conceit of the Amazon, nor Philoclea of the shepherd" (158). In contrast to the sisters' silence, Musidorus and Pyrocles have discussed their passions openly with each other and have plotted together to satisfy their desires. In fact, the princes have a much stronger relationship with each other than they have with their mistresses; they are at least honest with each other, but they have deceived the princesses in order to seduce them. They have worked together to separate the princesses from their protectors; thus, Pyrocles and Musidorus have increased the isolation of Pamela and Philoclea, while strengthening their bonds with each other.

This becomes obvious in the captivity scenes, which take place after Pamela and Musidorus have been apprehended in their flight and Dametas has discovered Pyrocles in Philoclea's bedchamber. When Pyrocles and Musidorus have been captured and locked in a room together, their first concern is their friendship, not the fate of the princesses. As they contemplate a sentence of death, they worry about whether their friendship will continue in the next life. Musidorus fears that "memory fails...and then is there nothing left but the intellectual part or intelligence which, void of all moral virtues...doth only live in the contemplative virtue and power of the omnipotent God..." (372). However, Pyrocles reassures him:

> We shall not see the colours but lives of all things that have been
> or can be; and shall, as I hope, know our friendship, though exempt
> from the earthly cares of friendship, having both united it and
> ourselves in that high and heavenly love of the unquenchable light.
> (373)

Only after this philosophical discussion of man's nature after death do Pyrocles and Musidorus decide that they must defend the princesses at all costs; Sidney does not use direct dialogue for this part of the discussion but summarizes it for his audience, which makes the princes' love for the princesses seem less important than their love for each other: "Thus did they...virtuously enable their minds against all extremities which they did think would fall upon them, especially resolving that the first care they should have should be, by taking the fault upon themselves, to clear the two ladies, of whose case...they had not any knowledge ..."(374). "By taking the fault upon themselves" suggests that the princes are being magnanimous—that the fault is not really theirs. Certainly they demonstrate no remorse for their plans to deceive, seduce, rape, or invade. Indeed, they speak most highly of themselves: "We have lived, and lived to be good to ourselves and others. Our souls...have achieved the causes of their hither coming. They have known, and honoured with knowledge, the cause of their creation. And to many men...it hath been behoveful that we should live" (371). In such self-congratulatory exchanges, Pyrocles and Musidorus encourage and lift each other's spirits.

Pamela and Philoclea behave very differently in their imprisonment; they hardly know how to talk to each other because they are not friends. In his essay "On Friendship," Montaigne says that

> the usual capacity of women is not equal to the demands of the communion and intercourse which is the sustenance of that sacred bond [of friendship]; nor do their minds seem firm enough to sustain the pressure of so hard and lasting a knot.... there has never yet been an instance of this sex reaching that point [friendship], and by the common consent of the ancient schools this is denied. (249-250)

Being themselves untrustworthy women, they are naturally too suspicious to become friends. Further, they are too selfish, being too wrapped up in themselves to concern themselves with someone else. Finally, they are not reasonable enough to discuss the weighty matters that occupy true friends. For these reasons, the sisters barely know each other. We do not hear them speak; instead, their rather short discussion is summarized:

> when Philanax...had by force left her [Pamela] under guard with her sister, and...the two sisters were matched as well in the disgraces of fortune as they had been in the best beauties of nature, those things that till then bashfulness and mistrust had made them hold reserved one from the other, now fear...forced them interchangeably to lay open; their passions, then so swelling in them as they would have made auditors of stones rather than have swal-

lowed up in silence the choking adventures were fallen unto them.
(368)

Pamela and Philoclea, like the writers of conduct books, believe that women are untrustworthy, so they have never confided in each other. They speak only because their bursting emotions force them to speak to someone—or something; each girl would have said the same things ("would have made auditors of stones") even if she had been alone in the room. Pamela and Philoclea share no philosophical theories with each other; the sole content of their forced discussion is their passion. The princes comfort each other, but Pamela and Philoclea only make each other more forlorn; they discover that "the one could not any way be helped by the other, but rather the one could not be miserable but that it must necessarily make the other miserable also" (369). Since Pamela and Philoclea cannot help each other, they resort, woman-like, to "crying and wringing of hands" (369). Finally, realizing that they can do nothing else, they sit down to write to their captors in defense of Pyrocles and Musidorus. Further, these letters are completely ineffectual; in the trial scene, the letters are given to Philanax, who does not allow them to be admitted as evidence, and does not even read them himself. Although Sidney includes the texts of the letters in his narrative, he makes it clear that Pamela and Philoclea remain in silent isolation. They never speak in their own defense. In fact, they never appear in the story again except through an indirect reference to the marriages of Pyrocles and Musidorus. Ironically, their silence, a feminine virtue much emphasized in courtesy literature, has helped their seducers to bring about their downfall.

Pamela and Philoclea are clearly the victims of Musidorus' and Pyrocles' lust. As Lanham notes, "The Neo-Platonism each hero affects is constantly belied by his single-minded concentration on bedding his chosen woman" (373). An Elizabethan might argue that the princesses never should have placed themselves in such vulnerable positions, but Sidney certainly appears to allot more blame to his heroes than he does to his heroines. He demonstrates that in a society which makes women's status wholly dependent on men, women have to guard their virtue very carefully; their powerlessness and inferior condition make them seem valueless to the men who control them. He indicates this by emphasizing the guilt of the heroes and de-emphasizing the guilt of the heroines. This is a deviation from the idea that women, as sources of temptation, are to carry the blame for their own seduction. Sidney makes Pyrocles more culpable than Philoclea by stressing her impressionable youth, her extreme sweetness, and her lack of experience in any but the most homely situations. Pyrocles, the hero, has travelled and performed courageous deeds, while Philoclea has been sheltered, her virtue completely untried until her parents effectively abandon her in the Arcadian countryside. Further, Pyrocles has plotted his course from his first viewing of Philoclea's portrait—before he has had a chance to be tempted by her sexuality. Musidorus is guiltier than Pamela because she, too, has been abandoned by her parents. She uses no wiles to attract Musidorus; she does not even dress attractively—and she is asleep when he attacks her. Sidney also emphasizes the vulnerability and isolation of both Philoclea and Pamela; they have no one to turn to except their lovers. Thus, even though Sidney sets his heroines in standard romance situations, his rejection of Renaissance commonplaces alters his readers' attitudes very subtly; he uses humor or irony to indicate the guilt of the heroes in their actions and intentions toward the heroines, who are little more than silent pawns, moved about at will by their parents and their lovers.

II

Although Pamela and Philoclea are little more than contemporary stereotypes, Gynecia's character develops through her relationships with Pyrocles and Philoclea and her juxtaposition with Basilius and his corresponding illicit passion for the disguised Pyrocles. Much of Gynecia's personality is revealed through her own words; she voices her feelings more often and at greater length than either Pamela or Philoclea, although, like her daughters, she has no friend or confidant. Gynecia examines her feelings more extensively and deceives herself less than any of the other characters in the work. Sidney also develops Gynecia through his observations about her which are sympathetic one minute and harsh the next. The frequent shifts in tone as he directs the reader's reactions to her may well indicate that Sidney has ambiguous feelings about the strong individualistic female character he creates, perhaps because he is just beginning to examine the realities of female character outside the bounds of convention which demanded that women be virtuous inspirations for men and denied them the right to err and repent. Sidney treats Gynecia much more seriously than he treats Pamela and Philoclea, although through his portrayal of her he still seems to be bringing stereotypes about the nature of women to the attention of his audience. Gynecia steps out of the passive role of the virtuous Renaissance woman to think, feel, and act like a man. Instead of being the pursued and wooed mistress, she is the pursuer and the wooer, becoming the inflamed lover pleading for mercy. However, Gynecia is not a stylized romance seductress. She not only repents, learns from her mistakes, and changes, overcoming her passion to lead once more a virtuous life, she also retains her respected social status. Her only punishment is her own self-knowledge.

Many critics have noted Sidney's emphasis on Gynecia, though without commenting in any depth on Sidney's attitude toward her, or discussing its significance. Richard Lanham remarks that "Gynecia is the one character in the *Old Arcadia* most critics would agree is fully 'third-dimensional'" (260). Zandvoort in his comparison of the two *Arcadia*s says of Gynecia, "Unlike the characters of Pamela and Philoclea, hers is almost fully developed in the original version [the *Old Arcadia*]" (89). I have not found any precedent in the romance tradition of the late Middle Ages or the early Renaissance for Sidney's description of inner torment and comprehension of sin or, in fact, for any psychological development of character; since romance traditionally revolves around the activities of men, Sidney deviates from his immediate predecessors even more when he develops in such detail a female rather than a male character. His sophisticated characterization of Gynecia may owe a great deal to his classical education. Certainly Euripides provides precedent for strong female characters. However, even in plays like *The Medea*, women are portrayed as either good or evil, and strong women, such as Medea, are usually evil; women tormented by passion, such as Phaedre, do not repent and change. Only in legends of saints or scripture are there women who repent, but unlike Gynecia, they turn from sin to sainthood. While Sidney may have learned his methods of characterization from the classics, his attitudes are certainly his own, and his blending of good and evil in Gynecia is unique.

Sidney presents Gynecia as a strong intelligent woman. All of the other characters, with the exception of Basilius, recognize her great wit. She has been virtuous until Pyrocles invades Arcadia, whereupon an unfamiliar and unreasoning passion overcomes her virtue and self-control. The combination of intelligence and passion makes Gynecia a formidable foe to Pyrocles. She is the only Arcadian who penetrates his disguise and discerns his entanglements. She recognizes his love for Philoclea and Philoclea's for him. She also knows of Basilius' love for him. Gynecia's intelligence keeps her always aware of the depths to which her passion is leading her, even though she does not learn to control it until catastrophe strikes. Indeed, Sidney departs markedly from romance traditions in his creation of Gynecia, the only character in the *Old Arcadia* who learns anything at all from errors in judgment and changes, processes left to misguided heroes in romances.

Sidney censures Gynecia repeatedly for her lapses from virtue, but he also sympathetically claims that her faults are representative human failings rather than strictly feminine characteristics, and he identifies with her. The judgment of Gynecia begins with the first mention of her. Sidney calls Gynecia "a lady worthy enough to have had her name in continual remembrance," but he goes on to qualify his first approval of her with "if her latter time had not blotted her well governed youth, although the wound fell more to her own conscience than to the knowledge of the world, fortune something supplying her want of virtue" (4). The use of "if" completely reverses the first complimentary words about Gynecia, saying, in effect, that she is *not* worthy enough to be remembered. This combination of praise and censure in the same sentence may indicate Sidney's ambiguity toward Gynecia, although the reversal emphasizes his judgment of her.

Gynecia's fall is caused by the onslaught of irresistible passion beginning with her first meeting with Pyrocles. Passion conquers Gynecia in much the same way that it defeats Pyrocles and Musidorus, through visual attack, although the process is more gradual for her. Pyrocles falls in love with Philoclea's picture, and one glimpse of Pamela conquers Musidorus; Gynecia likewise falls when she sees Cleophila, and her passion strengthens as she watches Cleophila kill the lion which threatens Philoclea. Sidney describes her feelings as they progress, like Pyrocles', from the first faint longings of love to a determination to "enjoy":

> at the first sight [Gynecia] had of Cleophila, her heart gave her she
> was a man thus for some strange cause disguised, which now this
> combat did in effect assure her of, because she measured the
> possibility of all women's hearts out of her own. And this doubt
> framed in her a desire to know, and desire to know brought forth
> shortly such longing to enjoy that it reduced her whole mind to an
> extreme and unfortunate slavery—pitifully, truly, considering her
> beauty and estate; but for a perfect mark of the triumph of love
> who could in one moment overthrow the heart of a wise lady, so
> that neither honor long maintained, nor love of husband and
> children, could withstand it. (48)

Sidney makes clear from the first that Gynecia's love is tragic, calling it "slavery,"
and declaring that he expects more self-control of a woman of Gynecia's "beauty
and estate" than he does of people of lesser attributes. He foreshadows Gynecia's
willingness to sacrifice chastity and family, the most important concerns for an
Elizabethan woman, in order to pursue her passion.

Gynecia's love for Pyrocles quickly destroys all her other bonds of affection.
She becomes merely indifferent to Pamela, but she begins to feel such chilling
jealousy of Philoclea that it finally amounts to hatred. Although jealousy is a
common characteristic of both the heroines and the villainesses of Sidney's
predecessors, Gynecia's emotion is out of the ordinary because of its intensity and
its object. It begins to emerge soon after Pyrocles kills the lion, confirming her
growing conviction that he is indeed a man. As she watches him during the
eclogues, she is stung by his preference for Philoclea:

> already was she [Gynecia] fallen into a jealous envy against her
> daughter Philoclea, because she found...[Pyrocles] showed such
> extraordinary dutiful favour unto her; and even that settled her
> opinion the more of...[Pyrocles'] manhood. And this doubtful
> jealousy served as a bellows to kindle the violent coals of her
> passion. (49-50)

Thus Gynecia's jealousy of Philoclea demonstrates the hold her passion has on her
even this early in the story, affecting all of her relationships, destroying all of her

self-control, and undermining her long-established virtue. Even though passion diminishes the virtue of all of the major characters, Sidney's audience would have considered Gynecia's even more reprehensible than the other characters' because she was a wife and mother.

The opening scene of Book II depicts a Gynecia already controlled by her passion, though she is still struggling against it:

> There appeared unto the eyes of her judgment the evils she was like to run into, with ugly infamy waiting upon them; she saw the terrors of her own conscience; she was witness of her long-exercised virtue, which made this vice the fuller of deformity. The uttermost of the good she could aspire unto was but a fountain of danger; and the least of her dangers was a mortal wound to her vexed spirits; and lastly, no small part of her evils was that she was wise to see her evils. (91)

The words Sidney uses to describe the depths to which she has fallen—"evils," "ugly infamy," "terrors," "vice," "deformity," "danger," and "mortal wound"—are stronger than those she herself utters:

> Alas, alas...if there were but one hope for all my pains, or but one excuse for all my faultiness! But, wretch that I am, my torment is beyond all succor, and my ill-deserving doth exceed my ill fortune. (92)

Gynecia's "faultiness" and "ill-deserving" are not as damning as the narrator's "deformity" and "Ugly infamy," and she is quick to mention her "ill fortune," which the narrator does not even consider; he dwells instead on her "evils."

Gynecia continues her self-analysis as she casts about for some cause of her misery beyond herself, while keeping sight of her own guilt:

> For nothing else did my husband take this strange resolution to live so solitary, for nothing else have the winds delivered this strange guest to my country, for nothing else have the destinies reserved my life to this time, but that only I, most wretched I, should become a plague to myself, and a shame to womankind. (92)

This speech parallels Philoclea's lament for her seemingly shameful love for the Amazon Cleophila, but the content of the speeches differs markedly. Philoclea blames only herself for her misfortunes, but Gynecia tries to see herself as a woman acted upon by forces beyond her control—her husband, contrary winds, destiny—as she abandons her accustomed role of virtuous womanhood. Gynecia knows herself very well, however; she recognizes that, even in the midst of her guilt, she would welcome the consummation of her passion:

> Yet if my desire, how unjust so ever it be, might take effect, though a thousand deaths followed it, and every death were followed with a thousand shames, yet should not my sepulchre receive me without some contentment. (92)

Gynecia does not act blindly in her love; she is aware of what is happening to her, although she is not able to control it. Richard Lanham notes Gynecia's recognition of "the absolute predominance of passion in her own behavior. She will do anything for satisfaction" (216). He also states that Gynecia's speech sets the tone for Book II, and that "It is to this level that the rest of the characters are to be reduced" during its course (216). Although her path is the one all of the characters follow, Sidney focuses on Gynecia's fall from virtue; he describes in great detail her struggles with love, while he spends little time discussing the resistance of Pyrocles and Musidorus, and allows Basilius to succumb at once. Perhaps his aim was to arouse sympathy for Gynecia. She is certainly less evil if she struggles against passion than if she succumbs as easily as Basilius. Society allowed husbands to be unchaste—an old husband adulterously in love with a young woman may not be evil, but merely foolish—yet a wife must be chaste above all else.

The second scene in Book II demonstrates the contrast between Gynecia's resistance to passion and Pyrocles' and Basilius' acceptance of it. Shortly after the soliloquy which sets the tone of Book II, Gynecia hears Pyrocles lament his unrequited passion. Not only has he lost his reason, he has no hope for the consummation of his love. He certainly feels no guilt about his desires, and he feels no remorse at all for deceiving the Arcadians with his disguise. When Gynecia reveals to him that she knows he is a man, crying, "Take pity of me, 0 Cleophila, but not as Cleophila, and disguise not with me in words, as I know thou dost in apparel" (95), he is "stricken even dead...finding...[himself] discovered" (94); he is overcome, not with shame, but with fear of revelation. Pyrocles gets some time to think when Basilius bounces by also intent on his new found love, another juxtaposition of Basilius and Gynecia:

> But as...[Pyrocles] was amazedly thinking what to answer her, they might see old Basilius pass hard by them, without ever seeing them, complaining likewise of love.... (95)

Sidney treats Basilius as a comic character—the foolish old man in the throes of love—while Gynecia is always tragic. In a typical incident, Basilius sings about old age and love. Then,

> [His song] being done, he looked very curiously upon himself, sometimes fetching a little skip, as if he had said his strength had not yet forsaken him. (95)

Clearly, Basilius does not feel any guilt about his love for Cleophila. His "little skip" is his way of pretending youthfulness, a comic betrayal of his folly.

Basilius' delight in his new-found passion is in direct contrast to Gynecia's torture in hers; he seems ingenuous and simple in contrast to his wife. Gynecia appears more important than Basilius; she is taken seriously, but Basilius is taken so lightly that one must force oneself to remember that this comic figure is the author of all of the problems in Arcadia. His silly attempt at secluding himself in the countryside leads to deception, and even rebellion. Juxtaposing Gynecia's tragedy with Basilius' folly also emphasizes society's greater requirement of chastity in women than in men; people could laugh at an adulterous husband, but an adulterous wife is a threat to the family—as Gynecia's abandonment of her children symbolizes. Sidney does not depart from conventional attitudes about the importance of chastity for women (his treatment of Pyrocles and Musidorus indicates that he would also insist on the importance of chastity for men); he rather departs from simplistic attitudes about the nature of women in his portrayal of Gynecia.

If a woman's chief virtue was chastity, her chief duty was to her husband and children; in succumbing to her passion, even without consummating it, Gynecia also fails in this duty. As early as Book II, when Gynecia begins to abandon herself to her passion, she repudiates Philoclea, seeing her only as a rival for Pyrocles' love. As she considers her chances of winning Pyrocles, she cries,

> No, no, it is Philoclea his heart is set upon...it is my daughter which I have borne to supplant me. But if it be so, the life I have given thee, ungrateful Philoclea, I will sooner with these hands bereave thee of than my birth shall glory she hath bereaved me of my desires. (92)

This bloodthirsty speech places Gynecia's lust for Pyrocles above even her more natural and certainly more honorable love for her child. Her hatred of Philoclea soon becomes so strong that she can barely tolerate her daughter's presence. Sidney uses chilling words to describe her feelings: "The growing of her daughter seemed the decay of herself. The blessings of a mother turned to the curses of a competitor, and the fair face of Philoclea appeared more horrible in her sight than the image of death" (122). She also recognizes that the passing of time has taken away her youth and beauty only to give them to her daughter. When Gynecia looks at Philoclea with these feelings in her heart, Sidney likens her gaze to the one "of disdainful scorn which Pallas showed to the poor Arachne that durst contend with her for the prize of well weaving" (123); if Gynecia could change Philoclea into a spider, she certainly would.

Gynecia's lust for Pyrocles consumes her whole nature, extinguishing even her femininity. In the cave scene in Book III, one which presents several contrasting views of Gynecia, Sidney, in an ironic parody of Petrarchan love, suggests her complete role reversal with Pyrocles: Gynecia takes the part of the aggressive lever, and Pyrocles, even more "womanish" with Gynecia than he is with the other characters, becomes the cruel and disdainful mistress. This is certainly paradoxical since *Gynecia* means *woman*, and the reader might thus expect Gynecia to represent either the ideal of Renaissance womanhood, a passive creature who clings to virtue above all else, or her opposite, the completely fallen evil seductress. Here, however, both men and women are controlled by passion, and they are equally

culpable.[4] When Pyrocles hears Gynecia singing about her passion in the cave,
her lament is so like his that he identifies with her: "O Venus...who is this so well
acquainted with me that can make so lively a portraiture of my miseries? It is
surely the spirit appointed to have care of me which doth now in this dark place
bear part with the complaints of his unhappy charge" (181). He decides to look
for the unhappy person who shares the cave with him, declaring, "I will seek thee
out; for thy music well assures me we are at least hand fellow prentices to one
ungracious master" (181). Pyrocles is devastated to learn that his fellow mourner
is the one person he has been trying to escape.

Gynecia quickly recognizes the other inhabitant of the cave and pleads with
him for love:

> How is Gynecia so unworthy in thine eyes; or whom cannot abun-
> dance of love make worthy? O think not that cruelty or ungrateful-
> ness can flow from a good mind! O weigh, alas, weigh with
> thyself the new effects of this mighty passion: that I, unfit for my
> state, uncomely for my sex, must become a suppliant at thy feet!
> By the happy woman that bare thee, by all the joys of thy heart
> and success of thy desire, I beseech thee turn thyself into some
> consideration of me, and rather show pity in now helping me than
> in too late repenting my death, which hourly threatens me. (184)

This is the kind of pleading usually left to lovelorn heroes seeking to persuade cold
mistresses, as in the Fourth Song of *Astrophil and Stella*:

> Only Joy, now here you are
> Fit to hear and ease my care;
> Let my whispering voice obtain
> Sweet reward for sharpest pain;
> Take me to thee, and thee to me.... (11. 1-5)

Astrophil cannot advance in Stella's favor, so in the last stanza he threatens, "Soon
with my death I will please thee." Gynecia's pleading is much more anguished
even than Astrophil's because she knows she has a rival, and she expects to be
repulsed. Although Gynecia is degraded by begging for love from someone who

is not worthy of her feelings, she never appears ridiculous, as Basilius does. Instead, she becomes more tragic and increasingly complex, as Phaedre is tragic rather than ridiculous when she steps out of her feminine role. However, Gynecia's tragic frenzy, unlike Phaedre's, abates before she causes permanent damage.

Pyrocles' response to this heart-wrenching anguish, so similar to his own, is completely cold and calculating; he cannot spare any sympathy at all for the mother of his love. Pyrocles replies to Gynecia's plea "with a full weary countenance"—he finds Gynecia's passion tiresome; Pyrocles "impute[s] it to one of...[his] continual mishaps to have met with this lady" (184). His answer to her pleas displays all the contempt and disdain of the heartless mistress who has not yet felt the sting of Cupid's arrow: "then must the only answer be comfort without help and sorrow to both parties: to you, not obtaining; to me, not able to grant" (184). Pyrocles' coldness makes the reader more sympathetic to Gynecia, even when she responds to him with a threat to ruin both him and Philoclea. Clearly, Pyrocles has misjudged Gynecia, failing to see in her the same determination for satisfaction that he, himself, feels—a natural mistake, perhaps, since Pyrocles would not expect such aggressive behavior from a woman with her reputation for virtue. This does not make Gynecia an admirable character, but Pyrocles' goading makes her subsequent agitation more comprehensible:

> O...how good leisure you have to frame these scornful answers! Is Gynecia thus to be despised? Am I so vile a worm in your sight? No, no, trust to it, hard-hearted tiger, I will not be the only actor of this tragedy! Since I must fall, I will press down some others with my ruins; since I must burn, my spiteful neighbors shall feel of my fire! Dost thou not perceive that my diligent eyes have pierced through the cloudy mask of thy disguisement?.... Believe it, believe it, unkind creature, I will end my miseries with a notable example of revenge; and that accursed cradle of mine shall feel the smart of my wound, thou of thy tyranny, and lastly, I confess, myself of my own work. (184)

Pyrocles at his worst brings out the worst in Gynecia; his contempt of her makes her reveal her depravity. In this speech, which demonstrates without ambiguity her monstrous side, Gynecia shows her intentions to be as cruel and selfish as

Pyrocles', and, although she has tried to resist her passion as he has not, she is as completely controlled by it as he is.

Continuing the role reversal, Gynecia uses no duplicity; she always tells Pyrocles exactly what she thinks and feels, in love or in anger. She is not very practiced in the deceit supposed to be natural to women. Pyrocles' first response to difficult situations, on the other hand, is to concoct another lie—an indication that he has become more "womanish" than Gynecia. When Gynecia threatens to destroy Philoclea, Pyrocles responds once more in the way that has become so natural to him: he deceives her, pretending to care for her. He appeals to Gynecia's basest feelings to obtain his goal—the enjoyment of Philoclea; he actually suggests that mother and daughter should share their lover's favors, and Gynecia is so desperate that she accepts the offer (203). This, truly, is Gynecia's lowest point. She has abandoned herself completely to her passion, giving up any attempt at reason or reasonable behavior. Nothing matters now but her own desire; in fact, she is in the same condition as Pyrocles, but while he fails to recognize his state, she is fully aware of hers. She says, "But alas, if I had the use of mine own reason, then should I not need, for want of it, to find myself in this desperate mischief. But because my reason is vanished, so have I likewise no power to correct my unreasonableness" (203). Gynecia does recognize the evil in Pyrocles' suggestion, but she submits to her baser self, and his.

At this moment of her surrender Sidney, instead of condemning Gynecia, identifies with her, and explains her action in terms of human nature:

> In this sort they both issued out of that obscure mansion, Gynecia already half persuaded in herself (O weakness of human conceit!) that Cleophila's affection was turned towards her. For such, alas, are we all! In such a mould are we cast that, with the too much love we bear ourselves being our own flatterers, we are easily hooked with other's flattery, we are easily persuaded of others' love. (206)

In this aside, Sidney does not tease the "fair ladies" about women's natural weaknesses as he does when he describes Pamela' jealousy of Mopsa. His sorrowful tone indicates his compassion for one who falls into the trap of the "weakness of human conceit," and his ambiguity again becomes apparent. Here, Gynecia is not the stereotypical evil woman; she is a suffering, self-deluding human being.

Sidney's departure from stereotype becomes even more evident when the cave scene in the *Old Arcadia* is compared with what was probably his source, a similar scene in the *Amadis de Gaule*; there is no compassion for the temptress in the *Amadis*. In Book XI of the *Amadis*, Prince Agesilan, disguised as the Amazon Daraïde, comes to Galdap, which is ruled by the jealous King Gallinules and his Queen Salderne, both of whom fall in love with the prince. The king soon goes mad because of his love for the unattainable and virtuous Daraïde, but Queen Salderne assaults the virtuous Prince Agesilan again and again. Like Pyrocles, Agesilan protests that he is truly a woman, and like Gynecia, Salderne first pleads and then threatens. She throws herself upon Agesilan as he is lying in bed, "l'embrassant de rechef, toute tremblant d'ardeur..." (204), and when that doesn't work, Salderne "se renverse sur luy & le baise delicatement, l'estraignant de ses bras par une demy rage, si fort que Daraïde en souffroit beaucoup..." (204). After fifteen days of this kind of treatment, Salderne puts Agesilan in a tower with an iron grill through which she, and she only, feeds him (205). Sidney has altered the characters in this episode in his *Old Arcadia*. In the *Amadis*, for example, Agesilan is an uncomplicated character who always acts from the purest love and the highest motives, and always treats Salderne with gentle compassion. He is without the deceitful and single-mindedly lustful nature of Pyrocles; Salderne, too, is a straightforward villainess, a seductress without the complexity of Sidney's Gynecia. John O'Connor notes in *Amadis de Gaule and its Influence on Elizabethan Literature* that

> Gynecia's sexual advances to...[Pyrocles] wherein she tears away her clothing and exposes her body, are doubtless derived from Queen Salderne's much more practiced efforts to seduce Daraïde. The differences are significant. Sidney intends Gynecia to be saved. She is a basically modest woman overcome by passion, and so she behaves like a passionate woman, not like a whore. (19)

The differences between the *Arcadia* and the *Amadis* effectively reveal how far Sidney has deviated from the stereotypical characterization of the romance tradition. Gynecia is a tragic woman—not an evil one.

Gynecia's redemption begins in the cave where she revealed her greatest depravity. Whereas interaction with Pyrocles in the cave brings out the worst in her, interaction with Basilius, again in the cave, brings her back to her senses. Up to this point Gynecia and Basilius are often seen in juxtaposition, as in the opening scene in Book II which demonstrates their differing attitudes about their passion. In Book III, just before Basilius and Gynecia go to the cave, Sidney again compares the two as they ready themselves for the tryst with Pyrocles. Gynecia decks herself carefully for the night to come, and catches sight of a gold bottle, supposedly containing a love potion, which "Gynecia (according to the common disposition, not only (though especially) of wives, but of all other kinds of people, not to esteem much one's own, but to think the labour lost employed about it) had never cared to give...to her husband, but suffered his affection to run according to his own scope" (224). Sidney points at a common human failing once more, mockingly implying to his female audience that they, too, are probably guilty of not appreciating their husbands. His censure of mankind in general and wives in particular once more softens his judgment of Gynecia.

Sidney goes on to analyze Gynecia's feelings: "But now that love of her particular choice had awaked her spirits, and perchance the very unlawfulness of it had a little blown the coal, among her other ornaments with glad mind she took most part of this liquor, putting it into a fair cup all set with diamonds—for what dare not love undertake, armed with the night and provoked with lust?" (224). Gynecia is experiencing lover's passion for the first time, and part of the attraction is the excitement of danger. Because Pyrocles has deceived her, her anticipation is pathetic and ironic.

The scene moves from Gynecia's tragedy to Basilius' comedy as he waits for his "wife" to fall asleep so that he can keep his assignation with Cleophila in the cave—not realizing that Pyrocles has already sent Gynecia to the cave and is huddled in Basilius' bed in her place:

> Having borne out the limit of a reasonable time with as much pain
> as might be, he came darkling into his chamber, forcing himself to
> tread as softly as he could. But the more curious he was [to see if
> she slept], the more he thought everything creaked under him; and
> his mind being out of the way with another thought, and his eyes
> not serving his turn in that dark place, each coffer or cupboard he
> met, one saluted his shins, another his elbows; sometimes ready in
> revenge to strike them again with his face. (225)

This passage has a broad comic tone similar to Ariosto's in the scene where
Ruggiero tries to get his armor off so that he can bed Angelica; Sidney certainly
expresses no sympathy for Basilius' plight, as he does for Gynecia's.

Gynecia finally comes to her senses when Basilius meets her in the cave and
thinks that she is his Amazon. She realizes that there is basically no difference in
the way they have been acting. Angry and frustrated because she thinks that
Pyrocles has betrayed her, she decides to remain silent and let Basilius continue to
believe she is his lover in order to find out how he happened to be there. Gynecia
has, for the most part, ignored Basilius since passion began to rule her. As she
studies him to learn the truth about Pyrocles' intentions, however, she begins to see
objectively:

> having given unlooked-for attendance to the duke, she heard with
> what partiality he did prefer her to herself; she saw in him how
> much fancy doth not only darken reason but beguile sense; she
> found opinion mistress of the lover's judgment. Which serving as
> a good lesson to her wise conceit, she went out to Basilius, setting
> herself in a grave behavior and stately silence before him, until
> he...did now...know her face and his error. (276)

Gynecia is learning and changing. Her awakening to reason does not reawaken all
virtue in her, however. She rather basely permits Basilius to believe that all the
fault is his and maintains her own reputation for virtue. By her silence, Gynecia
deceives Basilius just as much as Pyrocles and Musidorus have deceived the
Arcadians through disguise, perhaps more, since the princes are eventually

uncovered and Gynecia is not. Basilius' reaction, as described by the narrator, emphasizes Gynecia's hidden guilt:

> Therefore, embracing her and confessing that her virtue shined in
> his vice, he did even with a true resolved mind vow unto her that,
> so long as he unworthy of her did live, she should be the furthest
> and only limit of his affection. He thanked the destinies that had
> wrought her honour out of his shame; and that had made his own
> striving to go amiss to be the best mean ever after to hold him in
> the right path. (278)

The narrator, who has so often judged Gynecia in the past, remains silent about Basilius' belief in Gynecia's virtue; this has the effect of making the passage even more ironic than if Sidney had moralized about lost virtue, and the narrator's silence passes perhaps stronger judgment than if he had spoken. Gynecia's silence makes her more guilty than her passion did, since Sidney describes passion as if it were a disease caught unintentionally, but Gynecia deliberately chooses to remain silent.

When she sees Basilius fall into his death-like sleep after drinking her potion, however, Gynecia repents:

> Her reason began to cry out against the filthy rebellion of sinful
> sense, and to tear itself with anguish for having made so weak a
> resistance; her conscience (a terrible witness of the inward
> wickedness) still nourishing this debateful fire; her complaint now
> not having an end directed to it, something to disburden sorrow;
> but as a necessary downfall of inward wretchedness, she saw the
> rigour of the laws was like to lay a shameful death upon her——
> which being for that action undeserved, made it more miserable.
> (279)

Gynecia recognizes that she in fact did not resist passion as much as she could have, having substituted words for action. No word of compassion softens this description. Gynecia cries out, "O, there is no receipt for polluted minds! Whither, then, wilt thou lead this captive of thine, O snaky despair?" (279-280). She also repents of her unnatural hatred of Philoclea, but in the midst of her self-reproach she recognizes that there is still in her some spark of affection for Pyrocles; she acts as she avoids rekindling desire by trying never to look at Pyrocles. Gynecia has learned something about her own nature; she has changed enough not to submit to desire again (although this passage does signal the beginning of a new passion, despair). The remainder of love which cannot be extinguished even by the tragic death of Basilius makes Gynecia very real to the reader. She sees it for what it is, and manages to control it instead of allowing it to control her.

In the trial scene, Gynecia appears as a changed woman. She is dressed in "a long cloak which reached to the ground, of russet coarse cloth," her hair "so lying upon her shoulders as a man might well see had no artificial carelessness" and covered with "a poor felt hat" (376). Her garments and her disarray reveal her remorse. She is done with romantic passion and is anxious to suffer what she considers just punishment. In contrast, Pyrocles and Musidorus appear arrogant and convinced that they deserve no punishment. Pyrocles, at last clothed as a man, wears white velvet with a white ribbon in his hair, "in those days used for a diadem" (376). Musidorus wears a fine purple mantle and a Persian tiara (377), indicating his royalty. These young men seem to believe that they are above punishment; in fact, they claim that they should not be judged by Arcadian laws because "they were not only foreigners, and so not born under their laws, but absolute princes" (385). Although Pyrocles somewhat acknowledges his guilt as he tries to protect Philoclea, saying that he tried to seduce her but her chastity was too strong for him, he shows absolutely no sign of remorse for all the trouble he has caused in Arcadia. The contrast between Gynecia and the princes emphasizes her changed nature and their continued self-exaltation.

She is not passive, however. When Philanax moves to accuse her, she becomes her own prosecutor, crying,

> Stay, stay, Philanax...do not defile thy honest mouth with those dishonourable speeches thou art about to utter against a woman, now most wretched, lately thy mistress!....Thou shalt have that thou seekest, and yet shalt not be the suppressor of her who cannot choose but love thee for thy singular faith to thy master. (381)

At this point, it is difficult to think of Gynecia, having repented and desiring justice, as evil, but she is not the silent, submissive woman awaiting the judgment of the men around her that Vives or Geoffrey de la Tour-Landry, or even the Goodman of Paris, would have advised her to be. She is not acting with "womanly" courage which tends to be of the passive, stoic variety approved by Christine de Pisan; rather, her courage is active and heroic as she engineers her own fate.[5] She presents the evidence against herself and concludes with her own death sentence:

> There resteth, then, nothing else to say, but that I desire you you
> will appoint quickly some to rid me of my life, rather than these
> hands which else are destinied unto it; and that indeed it may be
> done with such speed as I may not long die in this life which I
> have in so great horror. (382)

Sidney admires Gynecia's courage and self-control as she stands before her accusers, her eyes deliberately downcast so that her passion for Pyrocles will not be renewed (376), but he criticizes the despair that has led her to confess to Basilius' murder (366-367). Euarchus' judgment of her cuts to the heart of her true crime, condemning her for breaking her marriage vows, "the most holy conjunction that falls to mankind, out of which all families, and so consequently all societies, do proceed, which not only by community of goods but community of children is to knit the minds in a most perfect union which whoso breaks dissolves all humanity..." (383). Euarchus, the voice of justice, has spoken for society in his condemnation of Gynecia, but Sidney cannot accept this blanket judgment of "the excellent lady Gynecia, having passed five and thirty years of her age even to admiration of her beautiful mind and body, and having not in her own knowledge ever spotted her soul with any wilful vice but her inordinate love of Cleophila..." (384). He saves Gynecia from death with Basilius' awakening; he saves her virtuous reputation with Pyrocles' and Philoclea's silence.

Sidney's refusal to punish Gynecia for her evil desires, along with her reinstatement to her former status, demonstrates that she is a changed character; it also demonstrates Sidney's recognition of the injustice of an idealistic cultural code which either placed women on a pedestal of virtue or sank them forever in iniquity.

Sidney acknowledges the irony of public opinion at the end of the *Old Arcadia* when he says that Gynecia ever after received "the most honorable fame of any princess throughout the world, all men thinking…that she was the perfect mirror of all wifely love" (416). Just as she does not deserve everlasting punishment, she does not deserve her spotless reputation; with Gynecia, Sidney repudiates the idea that women must be either saints or whores. He proclaims the real complexity of human character and the difficulty of correctly interpreting it when he adds, "so uncertain are mortal judgments, the same person most infamous and most famous, and neither justly" (416). In Gynecia, Sidney has stepped beyond the writings of his predecessors, according a female character the same latitude that heroes such as Ruggiero and Lancelot have, allowing her to fall and repent without condemnation.

Sidney continues his exploration of the possibilities of female characters with Stella in *Astrophil and Stella*, as he creates a lady who is not quite the ideal Petrarchan mistress; then, in the *New Arcadia* Sidney re-examines Gynecia, revealing, as Zandvoort says, even more sympathy for her (89). With Philoclea and, especially, Pamela in the *New Arcadia*, Sidney truly expands the limits of the literary images of women as he explores all the facets of their characters. But Gynecia, as Sidney develops her in the *Old Arcadia*, is the beginning of his development of female characters who exceed the limits of traditional Renaissance concepts.

NOTES

1 In her book *Gender and Authorship in the Sidney Circle*, Mary Ellen Lamb notes, "Sidney's inscribed female audience functions as a rhetorical ploy, to guide readers of both genders to 'read like women' in the first three books. In the last two books, all references to fair ladies drop out of the texts. In a deft act of reader entrapment, readers are led to judge not only the lovers, but their own readings, with the sudden intrusion of the rational (if sometimes inaccurate) perspective of a court of law rather than a court of love" (76). I believe that rather than entrapping the reader, Sidney prepares her/him for an ending which does not, after all, punish the guilty.

2 Margaret P. Hannay notes in *Philip's Phoenix: Mary Sidney, Countess of Pembroke* that Mary Sidney was just as much interested as the men in the family in the politics of the Protestant alliance between the Sidneys, Herberts, and Dudleys. She was also interested in literature, history, and chemistry.

3 Hannay explains that Sidney was quite concerned about sexual morality: "...as a commander in the Netherlands, Sidney sternly punished soldiers who had seduced or raped local women; he had come to realize that sexual attacks must not be taken lightly" (76).

4 Mary Ellen Lamb notes that "the way in which the...*Arcadia* depict[s] males as subject to passionate excess at least as much as females challenges the symmetry of the analogy that reason is to passion as male is to female" (83). Certainly, all of the lovers—male and female equally—lose the capacity to reason in the *Old Arcadia*.

5 Margaret M. Sullivan, in her essay "Amazons and Aristocrats: The Function of Pyrocles' Amazon Role in Sidney's Revised *Arcadia*," states that "On Basilius' death, the duchess becomes a spokesperson for both gender and state hierarchies. Gynecia is the sole woman permitted to speak in book 5's public trial because she uses the opportunity to support patriarchy and condemn herself" (67). I believe that Sidney is examining these hierarchies, but his refusal to punish Gynecia for undermining them may indicate that he uses her not to support them, but to question them.

Astrophil and Stella

Sidney drew upon a broad base of cultural and romance stereotypes when he created the female characters in his *Old Arcadia*; however, when he created the character Stella in his sonnet sequence *Astrophil and Stella*, he drew upon a narrower set of stereotypes derived from the Petrarchan tradition. Although Petrarch initiated this tradition, its conventions were adapted and codified by poets and translators of several nationalities. Stereotypical Petrarchan mistresses have gold hair, jet eyes, ruby lips, pearl teeth, rose cheeks, and lily brows. They come in two basic varieties: stony-hearted and cruel, or soft-hearted and pure. In Sidney's Petrarchan models, mistresses remain remote and unattainable and become symbols of either selfish cruelty or, like Petrarch's Laura, desirable virtue; thus, the dichotomous view of women persists in these models, even though the opposed stereotypes are more limited in scope. For example, the cruel mistress is not a seductress but a temptress who deliberately gains the hero's love in order to dominate him and keep him in servitude. She keeps him in a state of effeminate passion and inactivity. The virtuous mistress, on the other hand, is the personification of Vives' ideal, who guards her chastity to such an extent that she can barely offer a sympathetic smile to her lover. In either case, as in the romance tradition, the focus remains on the hero, the poet, and his emotional state as he revolves around his distant lady-in-a-tower; the emotional state of the lady is rarely considered.

However, as in the *Old Arcadia*, in his sonnet sequence Sidney does not follow his models in every detail; his Stella is neither the cruel mistress nor the plaster saint without feelings who inspires the lover with her untouchable virtue. Astrophil views his beloved differently than most Petrarchan lovers view their mistresses. He is not content to worship his Stella from afar; like Pyrocles and Musidorus, he is after much more tangible pleasure: like theirs, his end is "enjoying." As Astrophil speaks of his mistress as a flesh and blood woman rather than a remote ideal, Stella's personality begins to emerge and to change in a way that makes Stella seem much more human to the reader than vague and static ideal mistresses such as Petrarch's Laura. Although Sidney does work within the basic Petrarchan structure, his Stella escapes the stereotypical pattern; she has much more depth and vitality than Petrarch's Laura. The most interesting manifestations of Sidney's alteration of the Petrarchan configurations are the poems in which Stella speaks, where Sidney enlarges and develops her character. Sidney takes care to give the reader glimpses of Stella's personality as she gradually awakens to Astrophil's love, returns it, and finally spurns it. Sidney creates in Stella a complex character who is a real woman, not just an unattainable ideal.

This sense of Stella's reality has led many critics to discuss her biographically as Penelope Devereux, Lady Rich. Unfortunately, too many of these critics are willing to stop once they have triumphantly delineated the relationship between Sidney and the beautiful Penelope. In his article "*Astrophil and Stella*: Pure and Impure Persuasion," Richard Lanham accepts completely the notion that Astrophil *is* Sidney, who wrote the poems in order to seduce Penelope Devereux (107, 111). Richard Helgerson, in *The Elizabethan Prodigals*, expresses this opinion even more strongly than Lanham: "*Astrophil and Stella* is both the account of a love affair and the instrument of seduction. It tells a story, but is also part of the story" (144). He adds, "The attempted seduction of Stella-Penelope is Sidney's most flagrant abuse of poetry" (145). Others, however, note the biographical basis for identifying Lady Rich with Stella without insisting on a complete identification of the character with the inspiration, or on Sidney with Astrophil. Mark Rose notes that Lady Rich is the biographical basis for Stella but adds, "The fact is powerful, however, because it is dramatic, not because it is confessional. This seems to be true of all the biographical detail in the sequence" (22-23). John G. Nichols, in particular, refutes the notion that the sequence must be read as biography in *The Poetry of Sir Philip Sidney: An Interpretation in the Context of his Life and Times*:

> It has been asserted that, in *Astrophil and Stella*, Sidney's passion is...real...and the assertion gives us, in a nutshell, one of the commonest approaches to the sequence. It demands that for 'Astrophil' we read 'Philip Sidney', for 'Stella' we read 'Penelope

Rich nee Devereux', and as the central fact of the poems we accept that Sidney was deeply in love with Penelope. Apparently simple, this approach really raises more problems than it solves. It does not explain why the pseudonyms were used, it does not really account for the many sonnets which no one could describe as passionate (or, at least, it does nothing to encourage a proper appreciation of them), and—most unsatisfactory of all—it is derived from an unsubtle notion of the relation between a poet's life and his work. (52)

Nichols goes on to discuss his own approach to the sequence, which is to see it as a drama enhanced by Sidney's obvious use of biographical detail: "I see Astrophil, then, as a dramatic character, in the sense that he likes to dramatize himself and his feelings, and also in the sense that he should not necessarily, or lightly, be identified with his creator" (77). I would add that Stella, too, is a dramatic character, and "should not necessarily, or lightly, be identified with" the source of her inspiration. Most recently, Katherine Duncan-Jones has speculated that Sidney wrote the sonnet sequence for Penelope Devereux at her request, much the way he wrote the *Old Arcadia* for his sister.[1] This is a reasonable explanation for the biographical details that link Stella and Penelope Devereux and could account for the humorous portrayal—at times almost caricature—of the lover.

Along with the biographical examination of Stella, the other common approach is to examine her as the idealized Petrarchan mistress. Richard B. Young says in "English Petrarke: A Study of Sidney's *Astrophil and Stella*," "The 'virtue' of love for Astrophil is that it is true, a material fact and not a conventional manner. Stella is its symbol, and therefore the ultimate persuasion....She is his Idea, the formal and efficient cause, the producing agent and the form or essence of his experience..." (37). Thus Young places Stella firmly upon her pedestal.

The curious thing about most of the critics of *Astrophil and Stella* is that, like Nichols, once they have disposed of Stella's biographical or Petrarchan elements, they turn from her without much further consideration to examine Astrophil, on whom they concentrate. One exception to these methods of examining Stella is Nona Feinberg's feminist reading of the sequence, "The Emergence of Stella in *Astrophil and Stella*." Feinberg, unlike other critics, examines

Stella as a character in the sequence, noting that "Sidney's sonnet sequence invites a feminist interpretation because it not only shows a male poet objectifying the beloved in the way Petrarchan sonneteers characteristically do, but also shows a poet departing from lyric conventions to allow a female figure some autonomy of voice and character" (5). However, Feinberg criticizes Sidney for not developing Stella even more fully; she does not consider Stella within the context of the Petrarchan tradition or Sidney's other works. I believe that it is necessary to examine Stella as a bridge between Sidney's female characters in the *Old Arcadia* and the *New* in order to understand Sidney's developing ideas concerning the nature of women.

One thing Sidney does that allows him to focus more attention on Stella than other poets do on their ladies is to distance himself from the persona of the poet. Sidney distinguishes himself from his lovesick poet by naming him Astrophil; Petrarch, on the other hand, invites his audience to identify him with the poet. Sidney's distance from the sequence allows him to observe both Astrophil and Stella much as his *Old Arcadia* narrator observes Pyrocles and Philoclea. He often treats Astrophil's attempts to seduce Stella humorously, just as he does his lovesick swains' attempts to seduce their ladies in the *Old Arcadia*. And, although Kalstone claims that "visions of Stella...[are] fleeting, delicate, and hard to sustain" (167), I believe that Sidney takes great pains to develop the character of his heroine. Sidney's rather earth-bound view of love, with its emphasis on Astrophil's desire for physical gratification, leads him to portray Stella, the object of that desire, in more concrete and immediate terms than he could if he simply described her through the self-focused and emotion-filmed eyes of her lover. In contrast, Petrarch describes his love for Laura as a bridge between the sensual and spiritual worlds. Laura's beauty and virtue are, for him, reflections of divine beauty and virtue, and, eventually, lead his thoughts toward Heaven. Similarly, several of Sidney's sonnets describe Astrophil's love for Stella as a pathway to a higher spiritual level, but, like Pyrocles in the *Old Arcadia*, Astrophil is more interested in his mistress's physical than her spiritual beauty. Petrarch's more successful attempts to emphasize the spiritual aspects of love cause Laura to remain a shadowy stylized creature, but Astrophil's more consistent emphasis on the sensual aspects of love, as well as the intimate tone he uses as he addresses Stella, creates a Stella who is a complex character with a wider range of emotions than Laura's. A comparison of sonnets by Sidney and Petrarch on a similar theme, observation of women other than the beloved, demonstrates some of these differences.

Petrarch's Sonnet XVI begins with an extended analogy.[2] The poet speaks of a pale old man making his way to Rome to see the Veronica, the cloth which carries an imprint of Christ's face. Spiritual desire initiates the journey, but it is very difficult for the old man to leave his "sweet home where years have passed away" (2). It is only the need "to contemplate the image of the one/ he hopes to see again in heaven above" (10-11) that prompts the old man to make such an arduous journey. Like him, Petrarch forces himself to seek the image of his beloved, not in a sacred cloth, but in the faces of other women. It does not seem to be a pleasant task but the reward will be a glimpse of the shadow of Laura, and presumably worth the effort.

In this poem, Petrarch does not mention Laura's name, although he addresses her as "my lady" in line 12. This form of address lacks intimacy and effectively removes the poet from his beloved. Petrarch idealizes Laura and speaks to her from a respectful distance. The poet's purpose becomes apparent in the last two lines of the poem, and it is only in the last line that the poet refers to his love for the lady:

> So I, alas, my lady, sometimes roam
> to seek in other faces you alone
> some image of the one true form I love. (12-14)

Even in the last line as the poet speaks of love, he does not directly refer to Laura even as a woman; his word is "form." The analogy of the old man further distances the lover from the beloved, since the poet doesn't mention himself until line 12. The first part of the poem is entirely in the third person, and the poet describes a situation far removed from Laura and Petrarch themselves.

The tone of the poem remains very solemn throughout; Petrarch's language never sparkles with the joy and laughter of love. To him, love is a hard taskmaster. The imagery in the first four lines points toward the image of death that is more completely developed in the next four lines: "He moves, a pale and hoary-haired old man..." (1). The description of the desolate family left behind adds to the somber tone: "He moves...from the little family in dismay/ to think that now their father will be gone" (1-4). The old man is a pathetic figure who saddens his loved ones in order to achieve his spiritual desires. There is even a suggestion of death in line 2, "where sweet years have passed away," and it is echoed in line 4 with "their father will be gone...." Even though the poet does not specifically mention death, it hovers above this very old man making, perhaps, his last journey, from which no return seems to be expected.

The images in the second half of the octave add to the picture of decrepit old age. Petrarch speaks of the old man "forcing stiffened shanks" (5), "broken with age" (8), and being "by the road undone" (8). This is a description of an aged man near death, yet pushing onward: "he helps with his goodwill as best he may" (7). Line 6 accents the feeling of death in this poem, as the old man moves "through these last stages of his closing day." Petrarch's use of the word "his" in "his closing day" indicates not merely the end of any day, but the end of the old man's days. The desire "to contemplate that image of the one/ he hopes to see again in heaven above" (10-11) further emphasizes the feeling of death in this poem. Thus, when the poet evokes an analogy between himself and the old man, "So I, alas, my lady, sometimes roam" (12), one pictures him old, decrepit, and near death. There is no joy in this picture of love, and even the desire to see the form of the beloved in other women becomes a joyless wish, as indicated by "alas." Petrarch has no hope of earthly satisfaction; all satisfaction lies in Heaven, which is where his ideal of love leads.

The differences between Sidney and Petrarch are apparent from the beginning of Sidney's Sonnet 91. Where Petrarch begins his poem with a somber contemplation of death, Sidney begins with a sparkling vision of life. Astrophil addresses Stella directly, immediately, and intimately. She is a presence in the poem from the first word, and not as an idealized "my lady": "Stella, while now by honor's cruel might/ I am from you (light of my life) misled..."(1-2). Not only does Astrophil name her, but he uses a term of endearment for her, "light of my life." He also calls her, "fair you, my sun" (3), another affectionate description of Stella. "My sun" suggests some distancing from Astrophil, but in combination with the other epithets, the phrase appears to be little more than a flattering play on Stella's name; she is not a cold remote star, but the warm, life-giving sun, an image that brings her closer, rather than making her more distant. These affectionate terms make the subject of the poem, the poet's love for Stella, apparent from the beginning, while Petrarch does not even allude to his love for his lady until the last stanza (ll. 13-14) of Sonnet XVI. Like Petrarch's Sonnet XVI, Sidney's Sonnet 91 describes the lover's search for images of his beloved in the faces of other women, but where Petrarch compares the search to a spiritual pilgrimage undertaken with great difficulty, Sidney's Astrophil describes with obvious delight the beauty he has seen in other women while his "sun," Stella, is covered over with "absence' veil" (4). Because of his separation from Stella, Astrophil claims that he "live[s] in sorrow's night" (4), but, unlike Petrarch's aged and infirm old man, he still manages to find pleasure in his "dark place" (5), and it isn't spiritual pleasure. Astrophil is not concerned with heavenly images, but with warm, human bodies. His description of the beauty he sees in other women is not vague, as is Petrarch's. Whereas Petrarch mentions none of Laura's physical features, or even the word beauty, Astrophil revels in the specific and sensual:

> amber-color'd head,
> Milk hands, rose cheeks, or lips more red
> Or seeing jets, black, but in blackness bright.... (6-8)

These lovely features are all Stella's, but since Astrophil is not near Stella he must look for them parcelled out among many women. His thoughts as he observes other women do not fly toward Heaven, nor even immediately toward Stella: "They please, I do confess, they please mine eyes" (9). The repetition of "they please" conveys the strength of Astrophil's attraction to the women he has regarded with so much relish, and his words "I do confess" may indicate a feeling of guilt in the almost disloyal pleasure he has found in other women.

    It is paradoxical that Sidney conveys Stella's living impact through a sonnet in which Astrophil toys with infidelity to her, an idea that could undermine the reader's sense of their relationship; however, Sidney turns the paradox to Astrophil's advantage. The last five lines of the poem contain Astrophil's explanation of his pleasure in other women. His feeling that he owes Stella an explanation indicates that Astrophil does not perceive her as a distant ideal, but as a woman who may be hurt by his actions. He admits that these women please him, "But why? Because of you they models be..." (10). Petrarch ends his sonnet with his declaration that he "sometimes roam[s]/ to seek in other faces you alone..." (12-13), but without Astrophil's exclamation of pleasure, repeated twice. Petrarch has no need for Astrophil's "But why?" He doesn't seem to think that his shadowy Laura will care; at least, her feelings are not his concern in this poem. Astrophil is very much aware of Stella's human emotions when he says, "Dear, therefore be not jealous over me,/ If you hear they seem my heart to move..." (12-13), and he denies vehemently any true feelings for other women he may have dallied with: "Not them, O no, but you in them I love" (14). (Dalliance is indicated in line 13: "If you hear they seem my heart to move...") Both the reference to Stella's jealousy and the affectionate "Dear" make Stella much more human than Petrarch's Laura, left unmentioned until the end of Sonnet XVI.

However, Sidney's warm vibrant Stella does not emerge all at once; before Sidney develops the intimate tone Astrophil uses when he speaks of Stella, and before she becomes a dynamic character in the sequence, he employs the often hard and artificial imagery of the tradition to portray her and to describe Astrophil's rather artificial posture of courtly love. In the cycle's first twenty or so sonnets, Astrophil does see Stella as an ideal rather than a woman with a personality of her own. Sonnet 9 depicts her as if she were a statue; her forehead is "alabaster pure"; her hair is gold; her lips, "red porphir"; and her cheeks, "marble, mix'd red and white." In Sonnet 13, Astrophil speaks of Stella in heraldic terms: "Cupid...smiles for on his crest there lies/ Stella's fair hair; her face he makes his shield,/ Where roses gules are borne in silver field." Astrophil, at this point, has not conceived any real love for Stella; there is no physical yearning in the sonnets. He describes her not as a warm, loving woman but as a cold unattainable ideal as he speaks of her in the stylized terms of the Petrarchan lover.

In Sonnet 30, one of the overtly biographical poems, we begin to see a less stereotypical Stella as Astrophil's language becomes less conventional than it is in the earlier poems; he addresses her directly for the first time in the sequence. Sidney describes the buzz of conversation at court as "busy wits" ask Astrophil about such things as the Polish invasion of Muscovy (ll. 3-4), the religious factions in France (5), and the situation in Ulster, "Wherewith my father once made it half tame" (10)—a line which offers ammunition to those who insist on a strict identification of Sidney with Astrophil. Sidney places Stella in the midst of the babble with the last two lines of the sonnet: "I, cumber'd with good manners, answer do,/ But know not how; for still I think of you" (13-14). With Astrophil's use of "you," Sidney begins to change the readers' concept of Stella as a distant ideal fixed in the poet's mind to an understanding of her as an active character in the sequence. In other sonnet sequences, the lady never really comes into focus; she remains a creation of the poet's imagination. Astrophil's direct address of Stella brings her out of his mind and places her next to him in a social setting, focussing the readers' attention on the lady as well as the poet.

Sonnet 30 also demonstrates a change in Astrophil's perception of Stella as his tone shifts from artificial and distant to conversational and warmly intimate (although Sidney continues to include conventional sonnets throughout the sequence); for the first time, Astrophil speaks directly to Stella as a social equal. In Sonnet 40, Astrophil addresses Stella directly and even more intimately as "Stella dear" (2), although he still speaks of her as a remote goddess who regards him "from the height of virtue's throne" (5). Nevertheless, the intimacy of "O Stella dear" suggests that Astrophil will not be content to leave Stella suspended above him, too far away to grasp. As Rudenstine has noted, Astrophil's conversational style indicates that he does not see her as a distant ideal, but as someone on his own level (228). Sidney's leveling of Stella brings her to life.

Sidney begins to bring Stella out of the clouds and into the world as early as Sonnet 24 when Astrophil first provides the details of Stella's background; no longer does he see Stella as a distant star whose "heart is…a citadel" as he says in Sonnet 12, but as a woman whose life concerns him. In this sonnet, which appears to support the biographical approach to Stella, he rails against Stella's husband (in doing so he identifies Penelope Devereux, Lady Rich, as the inspiration for Stella). He speaks first of rich men who constantly want to amass more wealth yet still recognize truly valuable things which must be cherished—but Stella's husband is not one of these; he is

> That rich fool who by blind Fortune's lot
> The richest gem of love and life enjoys,
> And can with foul abuse such beauties blot,

Let him, deprived of sweet but unfelt joys,
Exil'd for aye from those high treasures which
He knows not, grow in only folly rich! (ll. 9-14)

With these lines, Stella becomes a person whom Astrophil knows and cares about instead of an impersonal ideal. Stella (not necessarily Lady Rich) is a woman trapped in a loveless marriage; Astrophil even considers it an abusive marriage—something as common in the sixteenth century as it is today. Sidney makes Stella's husband part of the backdrop behind her and brings him into focus from time to time in the sequence, adding drama to the narrative that develops; the poems in which Sidney mentions Rich are always highly charged. In Sonnet 78 Sidney uses harsh, violent terms for him as Astrophil calls him "a monster (other's harm, self-misery,/ Beauty's plague, virtue's scourge, succor of lies)," and the sonnet ends with, "Is it not evil that such a devil wants horns?" Astrophil's fierce tone in this line indicates his growing passion for Stella, as well as his growing frustration. He wants to "enjoy" Stella as much as Pyrocles wants to "enjoy" Philoclea, and his vision of her husband's mistreatment of her offers him a perfect excuse to invade another man's bed. The jealous husband in the background becomes a source of conflict for the lovers, making consummation morally and ethically impossible for Stella; at the same time, his presence highlights her chastity as she maintains at least physical fidelity to him. The conflict that develops is another leveling step which helps Stella climb off the conventional pedestal that keeps courtly mistresses separated from their lovers, as well as from the reader. When Astrophil and Stella debate whether they will go to bed together, they confront genuine moral issues; they become characters who encounter the same kinds of problems that people face every day, rather than an emotionally starved poet and the distant object of his love. In this way, Sidney breaks the stereotypical Petrarchan mold for both Astrophil and his Stella. However, since the Petrarchan poet always records his feelings, Sidney moves farther away from stereotypes with Stella than he does with Astrophil in his recognition that courtly love relationships, if they ever really existed, presented real pitfalls for women, who would be judged solely by their chastity.

Sidney continues to bring Stella out of the clouds and into the foreground when he puts her in social situations with Astrophil; like lovers in real life, Astrophil and Stella get to know each other through common social occurrences. In Sonnet 41 Astrophil describes a tournament that both Astrophil and Stella attended—a tournament of the type that Elizabeth enjoyed staging. While Astrophil took part in the tournament and won the prize, Stella watched and inspired him to do glorious deeds in the manner of courtly lovers. Astrophil says, "Having this day my horse, my hand, my lance/ Guided so well that I obtained the prize/...Stella looked on, and from her heav'nly face/ Sent forth the beams which made so fair my race." Paradoxically, Sidney uses a stereotypical situation in order to reduce the distance between the lovers. Stella is one of the people whom Astrophil meets constantly in ordinary situations—whereas Petrarch repeatedly dreams of and recreates his one meeting with Laura. Laura remains an ideal, while Sidney's adroit mingling of biographical data with fiction makes Stella become ever a more real—and less a stereotypically ideal—woman.

Further lessening the traditional distance between the lover and his lady, Sidney has Astrophil describe in several poems Stella's actions as they listen to or read poetry together. Sidney intensifies Stella's reactions as she listens to Astrophil's poetry but isn't moved (Sonnet 44), as she listens to another poet's love story and cries, showing emotion for the first time in the sequence (Sonnet 45), and finally as she listens to Astrophil's story and responds. Astrophil exults, "She heard my plaints, and did not only hear,/ But then (so sweet is she) most sweetly sing,/ With that fair breast making woe's darkness clear" (Sonnet 57). This intensification might be described as the softening of Stella. Poetry, more specifically Astrophil's poetry, reaches Stella's heart, allowing her to begin to feel the warmth of his affection.

Most unusually, Sidney's lady has a head as well as a heart. Although beginning to respond to Astrophil's love, Stella never lets her emotions carry her away; as a well-taught Elizabethan woman, she knows that Astrophil's gradually more passionate desires must be deflected for both their sakes; but since she is not a cold woman, her feelings begin to show, however much she guards herself: "Stella's eyes sent to me the beams of bliss,/ Looking on me while I look'd other way./ But when mine eyes back to their heaven did move,/ They fled with blush which guilty seem'd of love" (Sonnet 66). In this sonnet, Sidney brings into play commonplace cultural guidelines for women. As Astrophil describes her, Stella does not seem to be merely flirting or playing games with her lover; a virtuous Elizabethan lady, she tries to keep her glances hidden. Unlike cruel mistresses, she does not try to attach Astrophil to her, but unlike virtuous ones, she warms to his love.

This combination of response and reason in the lady is unusual in sonnet sequences. The poet usually is not concerned with the lady's feelings—only with her actions: did she smile at him today? Did she turn from him in disdain? Astrophil recognizes Stella's efforts to keep his love safely in check: "Love she did, but loved a love not blind,/ Which would not let me, whom she loved, decline/ From nobler course, fit for my birth and mind" (Sonnet 62). Stella is not a conventional remote mistress, but a woman who admits her love and cares about her lover. In her self-control, Stella is unlike the heroines in the *Old Arcadia*; passion never rules her, although it becomes more and more evident that she returns Astrophil's love with warmer than Platonic feelings.

As Sidney makes Stella an ever more active presence in the sequence, he changes the dynamics of her relationship with Astrophil. Passion begins to overcome virtue in him. In the traditional Petrarchan sequence, the poet's love for his mistress may begin on a physical plane, but it usually becomes purified and spiritual. The mistress becomes much too distant to excite the poet's blood. Astrophil's passion for Stella keeps her earth-bound for the reader, and clothes her with warm human flesh. In Sonnet 71 Astrophil cries out in frustration as he tries to reconcile his ideal concept of love with his real desire to possess Stella's body: "So while thy beauty draws the heart to love,/ As fast thy virtue bends that love to good./ But, ah, desire still cries,'Give me some food.'" The last line in Sonnet 71 is the pivotal point in the sonnet sequence and a turning point for Astrophil as Neoplatonic highmindedness gives way to powerful physical passion. In a sudden reversal typical of Sidney, he takes Astrophil's love, as well as Stella, the object of it, completely out of the realm of Petrarchan mental anguish to painful physical torment. From this point on in the sequence, desire gains the upper hand in Astrophil—just as it does in Pyrocles and Musidorus in the *Old Arcadia*—so that in the rest of the sequence Stella spends very little time on her pedestal, but remains a real presence in conflict with Astrophil. Although the next poems in the sequence again follow the Petrarchan love pattern, describing Astrophil's emotions as he steals a kiss from the sleeping Stella in the Second Song and Stella's anger in the next few sonnets, Astrophil's cry of frustration in Sonnet 71 lends new meaning to the old pattern, and Astrophil pushes forward in his physical approach to his no-longer-distant lady.

In the Fourth Song, which demonstrates with Sidney's biting and objective humor Astrophil's growing passion and desire for physical gratification, the development of Stella's character takes a major departure, both from the sonnets in this sequence and from sonnet sequences of other poets of the Renaissance: Stella's voice comes to the reader directly, without being interpreted by the poet/lover, although in this poem, it is not well developed. The song, in the form of a dialogue between Astrophil and Stella, contains Astrophil's plea for sexual gratification and Stella's consistent response. This is, perhaps, the most humorous poem in the sequence; it is a beautiful example of Sidney's ability to laugh at lovers—and, perhaps, at himself—determined to pursue self-gratification in spite of all obstacles—including husbands.

Astrophil addresses Stella intimately and urgently in the first line: "Only joy, now here you are/ Fit to hear and ease my care..." (1-2). His selfishness is apparent from the first as he centers on "*my* care." Stella is definitely not perched on a pedestal somewhere above him. In fact, the relationship of the lovers is now on a human—even commonplace—level. Astrophil does not want an idealized mistress: he wants physical relief. He makes no pretence of worship but gets to the point quickly in the next line with "Let my whispering voice obtain/ Sweet reward for sharpest pain," and in case she still doesn't understand, he adds in this stanza and all subsequent stanzas except the last his explicit desire: "Take me to thee and thee to me...." This is definitely not an appeal to a goddess, but to a woman.

Astrophil virtually bombards Stella with a series of practical reasons why the time and the place are perfect for "enjoying": the house is quiet and even "Jealousy itself doth sleep," Astrophil's notice of Stella's husband (10); there is a bed conveniently at hand (15); and her mother thinks she is writing letters (39). When Stella apparently starts at a noise, he quickly reassures her: "That you heard was but a mouse/ Dumb sleep holdeth all the house..."—Sidney's way of bringing in the little mundane cares a would-be seducer must face and reducing once more Astrophil's passion from Platonic heights to humorous reality. In stanza six Astrophil tries her with a favorite Renaissance seduction line, the idea of fleeting time: "Niggard time threats, if we miss/ This large offer of our bliss." But none of Astrophil's arguments has the desired effect on Stella; she is strong enough—or scared enough—to withstand him and retain her virtue. At this point, Astrophil changes tactics; he turns to physical persuasion, perhaps trying to embrace her. We know that she tries to restrain him because he says, "Sweet alas, why strive you thus?/ Concords better fitteth us;/ Leave to Mars the force of hands." Stella doesn't succumb to his caresses, either.

With all his fine arguments Astrophil makes no headway; Stella's answer is always, "'No, no, no, no, my dear, let be.'" We might think that four "no's" in a row should be strong enough to make him understand, but Stella softens their force with an endearment and the weak admonition, "let be." In the ninth stanza, after she has joined actions to words, Astrophil (unlike Pyrocles in a similar situation) finally gives up his pursuit. He says, "Cursed be my destinies all,/ That brought me so high to fall;/ Soon with my death I will please thee." This time Stella's reply has a new meaning, though the words are the same, "'No, no, no, no, my dear, let be.'" Now her refrain reveals that she cares for Astrophil (Sidney again uses the technique of skilful reversal at the end of the poem, here reversing the meaning without reversing the words), but her words still show a want of resolution. At this point, Stella is still fighting her battle, even though Astrophil has already lost his. She pits her virtue against her desire to please the man who claims to love her in a way that her husband does not; in the Fourth Song, she has not yet chosen between chastity and passion.

In the Eighth Song, a more resolved Stella speaks. In this poem, Sidney uses a third person narrator to relate the lovers' anguished conversation as Stella gives Astrophil her final decision. Here, Sidney's use of an impersonal narrator allows him to treat the lovers equally, again without filtering Stella's responses through Astrophil. Sidney's obvious respect for women serves him in his development of Stella's voice. Stella's speech in this poem is sustained long enough for her voice to be developed independently of Astrophil's; it rings out as clearly as Astrophil's in this poem—a major departure from tradition. Once again, Astrophil pleads with Stella for physical consummation of their love, but this time, Astrophil combines his earlier Petrarchan rhetoric of star worship with the language of the physical yearning of a man for a woman. Instead of speaking bluntly and prag- matically of his need and the available bed, Astrophil woos Stella with standard Petrarchan language that glorifies the beloved; he calls her "sovereign of my joy" (29), "star of heavenly fire" (31), and "lodestone of desire" (32), once more placing her above him. Unlike conventional lovers, however, Astrophil is speaking *to* his lady—not *about* her. This makes his use of the Petrarchan epithet suspect; he employs idealistic poetic diction in the deliberate attempt to seduce her. (Here I must point out that it is not *Sidney* who uses these tactics, but *Astrophil*, his more and more reprehensible character.) Indeed, he soon reveals his real intentions; as desire overcomes him, he moves to "Stella, in whose body is/ Writ each character of bliss" (41-42), once again acknowledging his physical desire for her.

In stanzas 14 to 16, Astrophil begins again to enumerate the reasons why Stella should give herself to him at this time, in this place, finishing his arguments once more with a move to embrace his beloved: "There his hands, in their speech fain/ Would have made tongue's language plain;/ But her hands, his hands repelling,/ Gave repulse all grace excelling." Stella's morals are still stronger than her passion.

Astrophil's urgent physical response to Stella is indication that she is not an unattainable ideal to Astrophil, and it also makes her individual personality more apparent to the reader. She is no longer the remote young girl whose virtue has never been tested, nor is she the shy, blushing girl first awakening to love. She is now a woman, mature in her love as well as her virtue. She speaks strongly and openly of her love for Astrophil. Feinberg notes the risk Stella takes in making her declaration: "In the Eighth Song, Stella's seven stanzas show a noblewoman taking herself to the brink. In articulating her love, she risks her own dishonor" (17). Sidney's Stella is very much aware of the social risks of breaking the boundaries set by Protestant Elizabethan morality. As Stella's words indicate, however, her love for Astrophil consumes her too much to be contained silently: "'If that any thought in me/ Can taste comfort but of thee,/ Let me, fed with hellish anguish,/ Joyless, hopeless, endless languish.'" She, too, feels the pull of desire; however, her denial of physical gratification is also strong when she confesses, "'Trust me, while I thee deny,/ In myself the smart I try,'" and again in her final speech to Astrophil when she pleads, "'Therefore, dear, this no more move,/ Lest, though I leave not thy love,/ Which too deep for me is framed,/ I should blush when thou art named.'" In this speech, Sidney demonstrates that Stella is not a stereotypical mistress, either cruel and demanding or distant and unyielding. She is not tantalizing Astrophil with coy remarks; she is deadly serious. She has very directly acknowledged her love for Astrophil and has decided on a virtuous course of self-denial. In a reversal of roles, Stella demonstrates the kind of reasonable self-control usually attributed to virtuous heroes, while Astrophil abandons everything he knows about Christian virtue in pursuit of passion. It is surprising that the feelings of the lady of an Elizabethan sonnet sequence are explored with such understanding and compassion. Stella is fully aware of how empty her life will be without Astrophil, but in spite of her need, she decides to maintain her virtue even though, at this point, Astrophil is not above exerting emotional pressure to get what he wants. It may not have been his intent, but Sidney reveals in this poem that he understands the psychological as well as the moral implications of adulterous love for women. In the Eighth Song, Sidney demonstrates that he believes that women are capable of both moral reasoning and moral courage.

Sidney does not end his development of Stella's character with the Eighth Song. In the typical sonnet sequences that were Sidney's models, the mistress does not change; usually she remains at a constant distance from the poet, and her qualities of virtue or cruelty also remain constant. But just as Sidney opts for realism in changing the distance between Astrophil and Stella, he realistically changes the lady herself. In the Fourth Song, she is a young woman whose virtue has never been tested; in the Eighth, she is a woman tested and mature in her judgment, and in the Eleventh, she changes again. Between the Eighth and Eleventh Songs are several poems which touch traditional Petrarchan themes of unrequited love; Astrophil grieves for his lost love, and notes that Stella grieves, also. He avoids Stella's company, but he watches her from a distance. He sees her in illness; he sees her with a pleasure party on the Thames; he thinks of her constantly. Sidney does little in these poems to develop Stella's character, but the sonnets serve to show the passing of time, as well as Stella's involvement with other people and activities and Astrophil's absence from her. Time is necessary for the final change in Stella's character.

In the Eleventh Song Stella speaks for the last time in the sequence, and, although her voice in this poem differs from the voice we have heard before, it is distinctive and idiomatic. This time, physical barriers as well as feelings separate the lovers—Sidney sets the scene at Stella's house, with Astrophil speaking to Stella through her window. In this poem, Stella seems to be world-weary, disillusioned, and afraid. Nichols speaks of "Stella's harshness to Astrophil" (126) in this song, and adds, "In Song 11, the positions [of the lovers] are in a way reversed. Here Stella, who speaks much more than she does in...[Song 4], is the petitioner, petitioning Astrophil to go away" (126). We do not see what has happened specifically to change Stella; Young charges that "the change in Stella has not been prepared for" (86). The first lines of the second stanza indicate that Astrophil has not sought Stella for some time; indeed, Sonnet 91 indicates that Astrophil has been seeking comfort elsewhere, and that Stella knows it. She seems to be surprised to see him when she says, "'Why, alas, and are you he?/ Be not yet those fancies changed?'" The word "fancies" seems to belittle Astrophil's love for her, and makes her sound disillusioned. Perhaps Stella is voicing her anger with a lover who has left her alone, but the following lines do not indicate any softening of her attitude, as there might be to reconcile a lover's quarrel, and "alas" appears to indicate her sorrow in seeing him. It actually seems as if Stella no longer loves Astrophil since she advises him in the fourth stanza that "'time will these thoughts remove;/ Time doth work what no man knoweth,'" and in the seventh, "'the wrongs love bears will make/ Love at length leave undertaking.'" These platitudes give a world-weary tone to Stella's voice, while Astrophil continues to address her with such endearments as "dear," "sweet," and "bliss," protesting his unchanging love. At this point, Stella is very much aware of the reality of her situation, while Astrophil still tries to preserve the delusion of sentimental idealism shrouding his physical passion.

One distinctive note in Stella's voice that demonstrates her sense of reality in the Eleventh Song is fear. As in the other poems in which Sidney uses dialogue between Astrophil and Stella, Astrophil persistently demands of Stella that which she is not willing to give; in this case, he wants some indication that she still loves him. While he stands protesting beneath her window, Stella tries to make him leave and reveals to him her fear of being watched, saying in stanza eight, "'Peace, I think that some give ear;/ Come no more lest I get anger.'" Though Stella cannot repulse Astrophil's advances physically as she does in the Fourth and Eighth Songs, she does so verbally, and, as Nichols says, "brusquely" (126) saying in stanza nine, "'Well, begone, begone, I say,/ Lest that Argus' eyes perceive you.'" Stella seems to know that she is constantly watched; the evil husband looms behind Stella as he has throughout the sequence. In stanza nine, Astrophil's last words in the Eleventh Song, Astrophil reluctantly agrees to leave: "O, unjustest Fortune's sway,/ Which can make me thus to leave you,/ And from louts to run away," so that Stella is finally left alone in the joyless existence she envisioned when she said, "'Let me, fed with hellish anguish,/ Joyless, hopeless, endless languish'" (Eighth Song). Feinberg perceptively comments, "In the end, it is no longer the hero's running away which moves us, but the heroine's remaining" (18). This poem has a dramatic quality that focuses attention on both actors; Sidney gives Stella equal prominence in this scene as he depicts her feelings in her own words rather than in the poet's agony over his cruel mistress. These are Stella's last words; in the last four sonnets of the sequence, Sidney once again shows Astrophil distanced from Stella and lost, uncomprehending, in his own misery.[3]

In *Astrophil and Stella* Sidney mocks the idea of Neoplatonic love, which could be a rather sordid excuse for adultery.[4] His real hero of the sequence is not Astrophil, who learns nothing in the end, and desires nothing but empty sexual gratification—it is Stella, who chooses virtue over passion and illusions of romance. Sidney creates the sense of a realistic relationship between two people, a dynamic interaction between lover and beloved. In doing so, he challenges notions about the nature of women and breathes life into Stella; she responds to Astrophil's love with all the desire and fear an Elizabethan woman—not a star—might have felt as she contemplated adulterous love. Further, although it is extremely difficult for a male writer to bring authenticity to a female voice, Sidney demonstrates his understanding of women's character when he has Stella respond in her own words and develops for her a voice quite distinct from Astrophil's. Sidney uses many of the Petrarchan conventions in *Astrophil and Stella*, and Astrophil with his introspection remains the focus of the reader's attention.

However, Stella is not a stylized Petrarchan mistress, an unchanging, distant ideal. Like Pamela, Philoclea, and Gynecia, Stella is a mixture of accepted feminine virtues and vices: she maintains her chastity, but she is inconstant in her love. She does not fit either of the roles established for Petrarchan mistresses: she is neither the cruel temptress nor the remote virtuous lady. The most important characteristic of Stella, however, the one that sets her apart from other Petrarchan mistresses as well as from other heroines of Sidney's fictional models, is that, like Gynecia, Stella is capable of moral reasoning; however, Sidney goes one step further in Stella: she also has moral courage. She demonstrates that courage when she deliberately rejects her love for Astrophil. Stella is a bridge between Gynecia and the strong, unconventional heroines of the *New Arcadia*, Pamela and Philoclea, as Sidney continues to explore beyond stereotypes the nature of women.

NOTES

1 Katherine Duncan-Jones has an extensive discussion of the Sidney-Penelope Devereux connection in her essay "Sidney, Stella, and Lady Rich" in *Sir Philip Sidney: 1586 and the Creation of a Legend*, edited by Jan Van Dorsten *et al.* (Leiden: Leiden University Press, 1986); she has more recently reiterated her theories in *Sir Philip Sidney: Courtier Poet* (New Haven and London: Yale University Press, 1991), 246.

2 Mortimer's translation of Petrarch's Sonnet XVI is remarkably accurate in its capturing of nuance and idiom:

> He moves, a pale and hoary-haired old man,
> from his sweet home where years have passed away,
> and from the little family in dismay
> to think that now their father will be gone;
>
> then, forcing stiffened shanks to stir again,
> through these last stages of his closing day,
> he helps with his good will as best he may,
> broken with age, and by the road undone;
>
> and urged by his desire, comes to Rome
> to contemplate that image of the one
> he hopes to see again in heaven above:
>
> so I, alas, my lady, sometimes roam
> to seek in other faces you alone,
> some image of the one true form I love. (27)

3 In his essay "*Astrophil and Stella*: A Radical Reading," Thomas Roche, Jr., discusses the Protestant influence on Sidney's development of Astrophil's character. This influence would explain Sidney's cynical attitude toward Neoplatonic love, which is, after all, adulterous love.

4 Legends of Sidney portray him as a pattern of virtue. Apparently there is some truth in the legends; Katherine Duncan-Jones says in *Sir Philip Sidney: Courtier Poet*, "In a period rich in scurrilous gossip, Sidney provoked no contemporary sexual scandal, unlike his brother Robert, who seems in the mid-1590s to have had a distinct reputation for amorousness and indiscretion....Ben Jonson in his drunken conversations with Drummond of Hawthornden revealed himself to be enviously obsessed with Sidney and his reputation, and would surely not have held back from sexual abuse if he could have thought of some....There is no reason to think that Sidney ever made a girl pregnant, as so many aristocrats did; nor did anyone in the next generation claim him as father" (181).

The *New Arcadia*

The *New Arcadia* marks the high point of Sidney's development of his female characters and his greatest deviation from contemporary cultural and literary stereotypes of women. In this revision of his first *Arcadia*, Sidney changes and expands the roles of his female characters so that they become much more prominent in the story, as well as much more active in it, than they were in the earlier version. In the first *Arcadia*, Sidney patches the princesses together from the collection of female stereotypes so readily available to him; in the revision, while he draws on the stereotypes, he looks beyond them to create complex and intelligent women capable of moral reasoning, who ponder topics like politics and theology, generally considered outside of the intellectual scope of women. He adds moral courage to Pamela's and Philoclea's characters, making them morally and intellectually superior to the others in the narrative.

In the new version, Sidney also develops a more serious tone for his story. Gone are the humorous asides to "fair ladies" which gently tease a familiar audience; the narrator in the revised *Arcadia* is less judgmental and more objective than the playful narrator in the first three books of the *Old Arcadia*. This might indicate that Sidney has envisioned an expanded audience, one which cannot be expected to understand when he is teasing and when he is serious. The revised work also places more overt emphasis on religious philosophy; while the *Old Arcadia* and *Astrophil and Stella* may be read against the background of Sidney's strong Protestant beliefs, the *New Arcadia* foregrounds religion in the Third Book, which contains primarily material not found in the older text. The serious tone of the revised work along with the new emphasis on religion make the alterations and added importance of his female characters significant contributions to literary concepts of women.[1]

Sidney alters the reader's perception of the already well-developed Gynecia, without changing her character much, by adding background material designed to reveal her motives and make the reader more sympathetic to her. He also alters the reader's perception of Gynecia by juxtaposing her with a truly evil woman, her sister-in-law Cecropia, who wants Basilius' throne for her son Amphialus. In the *New Arcadia*, Cecropia is responsible for all of the major disruptions in Arcadia. She is obviously a villainess, but Sidney does not merely make use of an accepted stereotype to fill this role. She is not a seductress or an enchantress, but a pragmatic Machiavellian schemer. He explores her mind and uses her to convey ideas about human impulses—not specifically *female* impulses, as he does with the other major female characters in the *New Arcadia*.

Sidney sets in opposition to Gynecia's weakness and Cecropia's evil Pamela's and Philoclea's strength and virtue. He changes the princesses in his revision more than he does any other character from the *Old Arcadia*. In the *Old Arcadia*, they are broadly distinguished by epithets and stereotypical behavior: Philoclea is beautiful and pliable, and Pamela is proud and disobedient. Neither speaks enough to have a definite voice. In the *New Arcadia*, they have distinctly individual personalities and voices, something that does not happen in romances such as Montemayor's *Diana* and Ariosto's *Orlando Furioso*. A strong bond of friendship and affection is established between the sisters, with the older Pamela nurturing Philoclea, except when Pamela falls in love and needs her sister's support. The princesses are so strong, in fact, that, with Amphialus, they threaten to become the focus of the story in the captivity episode, while the princes sink into the background as they ineffectually seek to rescue their ladies.

The plot of the *New Arcadia* follows that of the *Old* through the first two books, with much added detail concerning the princes' adventures before they arrive at Kalander's house where Pyrocles falls in love with Philoclea's portrait. Although Sidney adds many new characters and episodes, the princes still succumb to love in Arcadia and pursue their mistresses single-mindedly (although much more virtuously), disguised as an Amazon and a shepherd. Pyrocles' chosen name changes from Cleophila to Zelmane, the name of a woman who loved him and followed him disguised as a page. Pyrocles and Musidorus save Philoclea and Pamela from a lion and a bear in the *New Arcadia* as they do in the *Old*, but in the

New the rampaging beasts have been loosed by Cecropia who hopes they will kill the princesses so that her son Amphialus will be Basilius' heir. In the revision she also causes the rebellion in Arcadia. In Book III, however, the plot of the *New Arcadia* takes a completely new direction. In Book II we learn that Amphialus loves his cousin Philoclea; in Book III, Cecropia captures Pamela, Philoclea, and Pyrocles (still disguised as Zelmane) and tries to coerce first Philoclea and later Pamela into marrying her son. Through all of these trials, the sisters remain firm and grow stronger in love and faith as they resist their evil aunt.

During this captivity, Basilius lays siege to Cecropia's castle, and Amphialus engages in single combat with several knights, including Musidorus, while Pyrocles paces and frets in his locked room. At last, Amphialus learns what his mother has been doing to the lady he loves. He follows Cecropia to the battlements with his sword drawn; she sees the threatening gesture, backs away, and falls to her death. Amphialus believes that all his actions have led to pain for people he loves and tries to kill himself with Philoclea's knife. In the resulting confusion, Pyrocles finds himself able to act at last and sets out to rescue the princesses. At this point, Sidney's narrative breaks off.

His editors added the last three books of the *Old Arcadia* to the unfinished fragment in order to complete the story. Several editorial changes in the text bring the old story in line with the new, particularly when Pyrocles spends the night with Philoclea and Musidorus elopes with Pamela; in the revised scenes, Pyrocles and Musidorus behave virtuously and do not try the chastity of their mistresses. Although early critics of Sidney's work thought that the Countess of Pembroke either had made these revisions or had caused them to be made, Godshalk effectively demonstrates that Sidney made these changes himself; the revisions bring the actions of the princes and the princesses more in line with the virtuous behavior they display in the first three books of the *New Arcadia* (171-172). However, the *New Arcadia* remains a patchwork. Since it is not clear what Sidney intended to do with his characters when he stopped at mid-sentence, I will examine them only in the completely revised portion.

I

As shown in the second chapter, Gynecia is the most unconventional female character in the *Old Arcadia*. In the *New Arcadia* Sidney changes her very little; he does alter the reader's perceptions of her, however, by developing her background and providing motivation for her actions. Zandvoort says of Gynecia that "Unlike the characters of Pamela and Philoclea, hers is almost fully developed in the original version; and the alteration which Sidney thought it necessary to make in her case are slight compared with the rehandling of the passages concerned with her daughters. Such as they are, they seem to betray a certain sympathy of the author with the tragic figure of this passionate queen, a desire to uphold her dignity..." (89). Mary Ellen Lamb states that in the revised *Arcadia*, Sidney ennobles passion by making love "a motive for heroism" (108); thus, Gynecia's guilty love becomes less shameful and worthy of the reader's compassion. In the *New Arcadia*, Sidney certainly does not want the reader to condemn Gynecia but to pity her.

Compassion for Gynecia begins to build from the first mention of her. As in the *Old Arcadia*, her first appearance in the *New* is through the portrait of her with Basilius and Philoclea. In the earlier version, Sidney does not indicate any great age difference between the husband and wife; however, in the revision, he alters the audience's perception of her when he describes the picture as representing "a comely old man, with a lady of middle-age but of excellent beauty..." (74), thus emphasizing from the story's beginning the disparity in ages. Kalander describes the couple to the princes: "He [Basilius], being already well stricken in years, married a young princess named Gynecia, daughter to the king of Cyprus, of notable beauty as by her picture you see..." (76). Queen Helen describes Basilius to Musidorus as being "in his old years," and Gynecia as "a young and fair lady" (123). The age difference provides Gynecia with much of the motive for her actions, and creates sympathy for an attractive, not-yet-old, woman who is tied to an old and foolish husband.

Sidney also creates sympathy for the middle-aged Gynecia by juxtaposing her with Philoclea, who outshines her as youth always outshines maturity. In his description of the family portrait, he says that Philoclea "took away all beauty from her [Gynecia] but that which it might seem she gave her back again by her very shadow" (74); this description shifts sympathy from the daughter to the mother, since the daughter appears to deprive ("took away") the mother of the beauty that rightfully belongs to her. Later, Pyrocles rather callously echoes this poignant depiction of Gynecia's displacement as he speaks of his first meeting with Basilius and his family:

> His wife in grave matron-like attire, with countenance and gesture suitable and of such fairness (being in the strength of her age) as (if her daughters had not been by) might with just price have purchased admiration; but they being there, it was enough that the most dainty eye would think her a worthy mother of such children. (145)

Any woman with marriageable daughters would recognize Gynecia's position and would quickly identify with the feelings of envy and nostalgia a faded beauty must feel as she looks at her fair young daughters. Sidney creates sympathy not only for the once young and beautiful Gynecia married to an old man but also for the matronly Gynecia forever in her beautiful daughters' shadows.

Sidney further retouches Gynecia's character and builds compassion for her by emphasizing her wisdom and virtue, merely suggesting that her intelligence could lead her astray. Kalander describes Gynecia as

> a woman of great wit, and in truth of more princely virtues than her husband: of most unspotted chastity, but of so working a mind and so vehement spirits as a man may say it was happy she took a good course, for otherwise it would have been terrible. (76)

Typically, Elizabethan writers describe only good women as both wiser and more virtuous than their husbands; evil women may be intelligent and devious but not wise and virtuous. Sidney clearly intends his audience to perceive Gynecia as a good woman who falls. Zandvoort notes that "Gynecia's character is much more clearly defined at the first mention of her name in the revised version than had been the case in the original; and now the blunt forestalling of her downfall is in the *New Arcadia* reduced to the veriest hint. Instead of saying at the outset that she actually fell into sin, Sidney describes her as one liable to err should temptation come her way" (90). Perhaps Sidney's subtle changes hint at unfinished revisions in Gynecia's character that would have kept her from the depravity she falls into in the *Old Arcadia*. In the new version, Sidney attributes the possibility of Gynecia's fall to her working mind; he suggests that one's capacity for evil is measured by one's intellectual ability to distinguish between good and evil and indicates that Gynecia has that ability.

Sidney accentuates Gynecia's understanding with an addition at the end of Book I when the lion and the bear have almost slaughtered the princesses. After Pyrocles and Musidorus have killed the beasts, one of Cecropia's servants comes to apologize for carelessness, admitting that the beasts belong to his mistress. Although Basilius accepts the statement at face value, Gynecia understands her evil sister-in-law and conjectures that the event "proceeded rather of some mischievous practice than of misfortune" (182). But the true demonstration of her wisdom is that "yet did she only utter her doubt to her daughters, thinking, since the worst was past, she would attend a further occasion, lest overmuch haste might seem to proceed of the ordinary mislike between sisters-in-law" (182). Unlike the stereotypically faulty female, Gynecia knows how to hold her tongue; she is a wise and disciplined woman until passion overtakes her. As in the *Old Arcadia*, in the *New* Gynecia's wit makes her always aware of the folly of her passion for Pyrocles; this recognition of her condition makes her a tragic figure in both *Arcadia*s. It also leads one to question what Sidney would have done with her had he finished his revision. In *The Eye of Judgment*, Thelma Greenfield ventures, "If we are to guess about the unwritten conclusion to the *New Arcadia*, I will guess that the fascinating and heartbreaking Gynecia was the ace Sidney held up his sleeve" (119). It is possible that Gynecia, rather than her daughters, might have become the focus in a complete revision of the *Arcadia*.

Many of the changes in the reader's perceptions of Gynecia come from Sidney's juxtaposing her with Cecropia, her sister-in-law, who is the character nearest her in age and station. Even though Cecropia does not appear directly to the reader until Book III, she is a force well before that with her vicious attacks on Basilius and his family, and Sidney uses her as a foil for Gynecia very early in the story. Cecropia is the most single-minded character in the *New Arcadia*; she always acts in her own self-interest. The blatant evil in Cecropia makes Gynecia's passion seem much less culpable than it does when she stands alone in the *Old Arcadia*. Further, Gynecia's recognition of Cecropia's evil nature builds the reader's concept of her wisdom, even though she cannot control her own passions. Sidney always portrays Gynecia as an otherwise virtuous woman infected with passion, but from his first mention of Cecropia, the reader knows that there is no virtue in her. Nancy Lindheim states that Cecropia "represents a perversion of Reason....She is conceived in terms of pride, envy, ambition, malice, and cruelty" (151). Gynecia's transgressions pale beside Cecropia's.

Queen Helen of Corinth is the first to mention Cecropia as she tells Musidorus of her love for Amphialus, Cecropia's son. In her praise of her lover, she describes the excellent education he had from his foster father Timotheus and blackens Cecropia's character at the same time. She says that Amphialus had "as good education as any prince's son in the world could have, which otherwise it is thought his mother, far unworthy of such a son, would not have given him..." (123). From the first, Sidney describes Gynecia as a worthy mother of two beautiful and virtuous daughters, while Cecropia is "far unworthy of such a son." That the disparaging words come from the virtuous Queen Helen makes them especially significant because the reader has been led to respect and admire her. He provides further proof of Cecropia's lack of virtue when he describes the education she provided for Artesia, the daughter of a dear friend of hers. Cecropia "had taught her to think that there is no wisdom but in including both heaven and earth in oneself; and that love, courtesy, gratefulness, friendship, and all other virtues are rather to be taken on than taken in oneself" (154). Gynecia, on the other hand, is "in truth of more princely virtues than her husband..." (76), and she has taught her daughters to be virtuous in reality as well as in appearance.

The one apparent virtue which Cecropia has that Gynecia has not is love for her child. In the *New Arcadia* as well as the *Old*, Gynecia feels jealousy and even hatred for Philoclea when they both fall in love with Pyrocles, but Cecropia's plots all center on her ambition for Amphialus. However, even in this pairing of apparent virtue and vice Sidney has not followed tradition. Cecropia's love for Amphialus is obsessive, unhealthy, and self-centered. To her, the reason for having children is to have little images of herself to look upon,[2] as she explains to Philoclea when she tries to convince her to marry Amphialus:

> O the sweet name of a mother! O the comfort of comforts to see
> your children grow up, in whom you are, as it were, eternized! If
> you could conceive what a heart-tickling joy it is to see your own
> little ones with aweful love come running to your lap, and like
> little models of yourself still carry you about them, you would
> think unkindness in your own thoughts that ever they did rebel
> against the mean unto it. (460)

Cecropia typically sees herself as the center of the universe, and her love for
Amphialus is primarily an extension of her self-absorption. She does not really
understand love at all. Sidney describes Cecropia's version of mother love as
viciously as he depicts Gynecia's hatred of Philoclea. At least Gynecia's jealousy
stems from her passion; Cecropia's love for Amphialus stems from self-love. Even
her attempt to force Philoclea to marry Amphialus has its roots in self-love, since
marriage to one of the princesses would insure his succession to the throne and her
own position of honor in the kingdom. To her, it does not matter whether he
marries his beloved Philoclea or her sister Pamela; indeed, Pamela is the better
choice since she is the older and the direct heir. Cecropia thinks only of her own
lost position and Gynecia's exalted one; Amphialus must inherit for her to regain
her lost status. The thought that Gynecia's line will rule over hers constantly
assaults her monstrous ego. Cecropia's pride even leads her to deny the existence
of God; she places all her faith in her own powers. This blasphemy would
completely explain her wickedness to Sidney's Christian audience.

Cecropia is not a seductress like Ariosto's Alcyna; she uses no feminine
wiles and magical powers to obtain her ends. Rather, she uses her intelligence and
amorality to achieve her goals. She doesn't lure; she captures. She doesn't seduce;
she attacks. Only in her death does she resemble conventional literary figures; her
end resembles the Knight of the Tower's treatment of unbelievers in the stories he
uses to induce piety in his daughters: she dies horribly as she flees in fear of her
own son. Next to Cecropia with her predatory ambition, Gynecia seems to be, if
not innocent, at least a victim. We can easily believe that in the *New Arcadia*,
Sidney intended to continue his unusual and sympathetic treatment of this would-be
adulteress, preserving her reputation and allowing her another chance at virtue.

II

Although Sidney merely retouches his depiction of Gynecia, he makes major changes in his development of Pamela and Philoclea. Zandvoort states that "One of the most remarkable features of the *New Arcadia* is the deliberate and subtle retouching of the figures of the two sisters, showing that between the two versions Sidney had made great progress in psychological insight and artistic skill"(74). Zandvoort's "retouching" understates the major character reshaping that Sidney accomplishes in the *New Arcadia*. In the revision he creates in Pamela and Philoclea strong, complex characters. Greenfield notes that "Sidney created his two heroines according to familiar romance patterns...a conventionally contrasted pair of women projecting differences typically visible and temperamental....The contrast usually shows, as it does in the *New Arcadia*, an appealing example of clinging feminine beauty against a handsome figure of dignity and command" (37). In the works of Sidney's predecessors, contrasted pairs of heroines appear serially rather than simultaneously, when heroes move from one episode to another as in the *Amadis* or *Orlando Furioso*. Sidney alters the convention when he introduces his heroines together, and he subtly alters the convention by having his strong heroine, Pamela, cling to her weaker sister in certain situations. In the *Old Arcadia*, Sidney uses stereotypes to show how Philoclea's innocence and humility lead her to lose her virginity to Pyrocles, and Pamela's pride in her majesty leads her to disobey her father. In the *New*, both sisters have moral courage enough to resist all temptations.

Sidney's changes in Pamela and Philoclea become apparent soon after he introduces them in the *New Arcadia*. Perhaps the most appealing development is their supportive and friendly relationship with each other. The most obvious alteration in them is that they speak much more than they do in the *Old Arcadia*, especially to each other, and Sidney individualizes both the content and the style of their speech. The most unusual alteration in Pamela and Philoclea is their strengthened virtue, which is not merely a passive acceptance of fate coupled with unthinking obedience, but an active attack on vice. This quality makes them resemble the heroes—not the heroines—of Sidney's predecessors. In the captivity episode, Cecropia tests the virtue of the princesses, and they grow strong enough to resist the many temptations and withstand the torments that she devises for them.

Pamela, especially, demonstrates that her faith in God is the root of both her strength and her virtue as she attacks Cecropia, her weapon being articulate moral reasoning.

True friendship is usually reserved for men in medieval and Renaissance literature; it requires equality of station, intelligence, and constancy. Most heroines remain in their own homes; those who roam the countryside in search of champions generally travel with servants as their only companions. In either situation, they have few chances to spend much time with other women of the same rank. Most of the relationships between women portrayed in previous works, therefore, are not between equals.[3] Another bar to friendship between women is the lack of enough wit to consider the kinds of weighty matters friends discuss, as Pyrocles and Musidorus discuss the survival of friendship after death in the *Old Arcadia*. Finally, women in romance do not ordinarily develop strong bonds of friendship because they are changeable and unable to maintain constancy under hardship. Yet in Pamela and Philoclea Sidney shows true friendship, gradually established and then maintained.

The concept of natural family affection grows with descriptions of family parties in the Arcadian countryside. In one of these scenes, Pamela and Philoclea enjoy each other's company as they fish, making "pretty wagers...which could soonest beguile silly fishes..." (152). After several of these minor indications of family unity, Sidney places Pamela and Philoclea in a situation which leads to shared confidences. In this scene, Gynecia sends Philoclea to spend the night with Pamela under Miso's surveillance because she has injured her shoulder and cannot keep her daughter from Pyrocles herself. Philoclea finds Pamela in a dejected pose because she has fallen in love with Musidorus, who is disguised as a shepherd. Pamela, the elder, has previously taken the lead in the relationship; Philoclea says, "O my Pamela—who are to me a sister in nature, a mother in counsel, a princess by the law of our country, and (which name methinks of all other is the dearest) a friend by my choice and your favour..." (245). With "a mother in counsel" Philoclea recognizes Pamela as her mentor, and with "a princess by...law" she recognizes her as her superior in rank. However, the progression of her ideas indicates that the bond of friendship is more important than the blood tie. Philoclea appears to see the other bonds as arising naturally out of family background and age differences, but she emphasizes the choice involved in friendship; that they have chosen to be friends indicates the relative equality of the sisters.

Sidney usually portrays Pamela as the wiser of the sisters, but when Philoclea spends the night with her, he proves that the younger sister has a sensitivity that is a form of wisdom. Although Pamela is the wiser in politics and theology, Philoclea is the wiser in love, as Sidney indicates in this intimate scene. In Sidney's predecessors and in his *Old Arcadia*, the heroines usually concern themselves only with their own problems; in the revised *Arcadia* the heroines are sensitive women who share their feelings and ideas, and who reveal considerable intellectual powers.

From the beginning of the *New Arcadia* Sidney describes the sisters' loyalty not only to their lovers but to each other. They comfort and encourage each other in captivity whenever they can, and each expresses a willingness to die in the other's place (distinguishing aspects of Pyrocles' and Musidorus' friendship in the *Old Arcadia*). Neither sister will consider marrying Amphialus in order to gain freedom because neither will abandon her lover; the sisters do not break even under torture. Because her principles will not allow her to lie, Philoclea refuses to appear to soften toward Amphialus even though Pyrocles counsels her to be devious. Further, neither Pamela nor Philoclea will join Artesia in her treacherous plan to overthrow Cecropia because they refuse to compromise their principles. Thus, Sidney demonstrates the constancy of the sisters in friendship, in love, and in principle.

As Sidney develops the sisters' relationship, he also takes pains to distinguish them, much more than he does Pyrocles and Musidorus, and yet their situations are much the same. Pyrocles and Musidorus were educated together, as were Pamela and Philoclea; they go through many adventures together, as do Pamela and Philoclea; they fall in love at about the same time, as do Pamela and Philoclea; but Sidney makes only minor distinctions between the personalities of the princes, while he makes much greater distinctions between the princesses. Sidney begins to individualize the characters of the princesses from his first mention of them in the *New Arcadia*. Kalander describes them to Musidorus using phrases of the narrator in the *Old Arcadia*: "The elder is named Pamela, by many men not deemed inferior to her sister" (76). In the *New Arcadia*, Sidney has Kalander add,

> For my part, when I marked them both, methought there was...
> more sweetness in Philoclea but more majesty in Pamela...;
> methought Philoclea's beauty only persuaded, but so persuaded as
> all hearts must yield; Pamela's beauty used violence and such
> violence as no heart could resist; and it seems that such proportion
> is between their minds: Philoclea so bashful, as though her
> excellencies had stolen into her before she was aware; so humble,
> that she will put all pride out of countenance; in sum, such
> proceeding as will stir hope but teach hope good manners; Pamela
> of high thoughts, who avoids not pride with not knowing her
> excellencies, but by making that one of her excellencies to be void
> of pride; her mother's wisdom, greatness, nobility, but I can guess
> aright—knit with a more constant temper. (76)

Sidney develops these distinctions carefully throughout his revision. Lindheim
notes that "contrast is part of the...principle of Sidney's revision of his *Arcadia*,
and contrast in turn calls for some kind of equality between opposing members"
(31), so that in the *New Arcadia*, Pamela becomes more important where Philoclea
is the more remarkable in the *Old*.

Part of their complexity stems from their speech. In the *Old Arcadia*, the
princesses speak very little. In the *New*, they become articulate. Ann Dobyns
notes that in the *New Arcadia*, characters representing similar societal types
demonstrate similar speech patterns, adding that "because Philoclea and Pamela are
both princesses who exemplify the appropriate manners of ladies of nobility, their
speech patterns bear a number of shared characteristics" (92). She observes that
both princesses use a great deal of parallelism, and they both "generally employ
metaphor or figurative language..." (95). She adds, however, that "one way Sidney
delineates subtle differences between the sisters as philosophical types is by
assigning each a unique style of speaking with contrasting diction, syntax, and
form" (96). She further notes that

> For Beauty, Sidney develops a gentle and courteous, frequently
> hesitant style; for Majesty, an emphatic, self-confident style. In
> similar contexts, for instance, Philoclea will use a simple, un-
> adorned style, Pamela a highly ornamented style; likewise,

> Philoclea will use passive voice and subjunctives where her sister
> will use active voice and imperatives... (96).

These characteristics generally hold true for the princesses' speeches. However, Pamela and Philoclea react to situations as distinct individuals rather than as stereotypes, and their speech patterns reflect these different reactions. For example, whenever Pamela thinks of her love for Musidorus, the sisters change places, Pamela becoming the indecisive sister and Philoclea the strong guiding sister. When this happens, Pamela's speech patterns become hesitant and Philoclea's emphatic. This reversal first occurs when Pamela confesses her love for Musidorus to Philoclea as they spend the night together. Philoclea comes upon Pamela sitting in her chair with her head thrown back in dejection. Her very position demonstrates that Majesty does not feel very majestic at the moment. Philoclea coaxes her to unburden herself, but Pamela blushes, sighs, and falters; her agitated, disorganized speech reflects her inner turmoil:

> I pray you...sweet Philoclea, let us talk of some other thing: and
> tell me whether you did ever see anything so amended as our
> pastoral sports be since that Dorus came hither? (245)

Pamela's apparently abrupt change of subject betrays her to Philoclea. In her present emotional state, however, she begins her speech weakly with the imploring words, "I pray you" and "let us talk," and an affectionate epithet, "sweet Philoclea," begging her sister not to inquire too closely into her feelings. This in itself is unusual, because Pamela does not beg, even under torture. Her abrupt transition when she starts to speak of Dorus gives her away to her discerning sister. Philoclea tests Pamela: "I marvel how he can frame himself to hide so rare gifts under such a block as Dametas" (245). Pamela cannot help responding:

> Ah...if you knew the cause: but no more do I neither; and to say
> truth—but Lord, how are we fallen to talk of this fellow? And yet
> indeed if you were sometimes with me to mark him while Dametas
> reads his rustic lecture unto him how to feed his beasts, how to
> make the manger handsome for his oxen...giving him rules of a
> herdman though he pretend to make him a shepherd—to see all the

> while with what a grace (which seems to set a crown upon his base
> estate) he can descend   to those poor matters, certainly you
> would—but to what serves this? No doubt we were better sleep
> than talk of these idle matters. (245-246)

Pamela can barely complete a sentence when she speaks of Musidorus, and her speech soon reveals the extent of her emotional turbulence. First she loses control and admits that she knows something that Philoclea does not about the new shepherd in Arcadia: "If you knew the cause"; she quickly catches herself with "but no more do I neither." She turns again with "and to say truth...." She contradicts herself and uses two incomplete clauses, breaking off abruptly as if to change the subject yet again, and indicating that she has no control over her thoughts: "but Lord, how are we fallen to talk of this fellow?" Another abrupt turn brings her back to Musidorus with "And yet...." She makes an attempt to gain control of her emotions and her speech with "No doubt we were better sleep...," but she has already revealed herself. Pamela's disordered mind and halting speech are unlike her; they reveal the dignified heroine's tender side.[4]

Although Philoclea usually follows Pamela's lead, she quickly takes charge in this conversation once she recognizes the feelings compelling her sister's rambling speech. She says in short, forceful, and complete sentences, "Ah my Pamela...I have caught you. The constancy of your wit was not wont to bring forth such disjointed speeches. You love. Dissemble no further" (246). Philoclea borrows Pamela's "emphatic, self confident style" to confront her sister. She does not question; she asserts, "You love." In most situations, Philoclea does not use the imperative without a softening "let," as when she implores Amphialus to release her from captivity with "let not my fortune be disgraced...let not my heart waste itself..." (450); however, she commands her sister, "Dissemble no further." Philoclea has assumed control of this situation in a reversal of roles that demonstrates the complexity of both sisters.

In contrast with Pamela's uncharacteristic lack of confidence, Philoclea moves forward into love fully articulate and clear-headed, even though she believes that she loves a woman, Zelmane, and has no chance for happiness. When Pamela falls asleep comforted, Philoclea compares her own situation to her sister's:

Alas, she weeps because she would be no sooner happy: I weep
because I can never be happy. Her tears flow from pity; mine
from being too far lower than the reach of pity. Yet do I not envy
thee, dear Pamela, I do not envy thee: Only I could wish that
being thy sister in nature, I were not so far off akin in fortune.
(251)

Although Pamela fights falling in love and feels herself to be constantly on edge
in this new situation, Philoclea embraces love and moves forward to meet it. Once
she accepts the fact of her love for Pyrocles/Zelmane, she does not turn from it, as
Pamela turns from her love for Musidorus. She compares her seemingly hopeless
situation with Pamela's in lyrical parallel and antithetical phrases which reflect her
willing acceptance of her new emotional state. In love, Philoclea has become the
stronger sister, and Pamela leans on her.

The distinction between Pamela and Philoclea continues in the captivity
scene as they stubbornly refuse to break under Cecropia's torture. Pamela even
fights back verbally, a break from the tradition of silently suffering damsels in
distress.[5] In romance tradition women like Griselda and Chloe tend to grow strong
in adversity, but their strength is usually passive, more a stoic acceptance of fate
than an active resistance to their tormentors. At times they may use their native
devious tendencies to escape, as Chariclea does in the *Aethiopian History*. Time
after time Theagenes turns to her for clever lies that will save them from horrible
fates. Being male, and therefore bound to be honorable, he does not have the
ability to formulate lies himself, although he does not seem to mind acting on
Chariclea's. Like Theagenes, Pamela and Philoclea do not lie, even when Artesia
and Pyrocles present opportunities. For Elizabethan ladies and romance heroines,
honor was equated with chastity; however, in Pamela and Philoclea, Sidney creates
heroines who have the same moral courage and concept of honor as romance
heroes.

Philoclea appears to be the weaker and more passive of the sisters when she
is in captivity because she allows her distress to show in her careless dress and
uncombed hair, and she speaks to her captors softly and respectfully. When
Cecropia spies on her through her half-open door, she notes that Philoclea is
"sitting low upon a cushion in such a given-over manner that one would have

thought silence, solitariness and melancholy were come there under the ensign of mishap, to conquer delight and drive him from his natural seat of beauty" (457). As she watches the obviously grief-stricken princess, Philoclea's "tears came dropping down like rain in sunshine" (457).   Cecropia mistakenly assumes that Philoclea's tears and distress indicate moral weakness and vulnerability. Because Philoclea loves Pyrocles, she is not even tempted to yield to Cecropia's falsely sweet persuasion. Cecropia calls her "sweet niece" and "dear niece" over and over again as she tries to persuade Philoclea to marry Amphialus. She stresses the family relationship with false affection, but the effect of this emphasis is to demonstrate her authority over her younger relative.   Philoclea gently but persistently insists that she has made a vow of chastity and continues to be immovable no matter what arguments Cecropia presents in favor of the joys of marriage, and in spite of persuasions in the form of gifts and soft sorrowful music played at her window. Cecropia soon becomes frustrated; the princess has an iron core of resolve hidden beneath her "sweet and humble" (465) outward appearance.

Pamela's composed exterior, on the other hand, hides her love for Musidorus. Although her virtue becomes increasingly stronger as her trials become more difficult, love continues to weaken her. She does not fear for her own safety; she forcefully and resolutely resists Cecropia. Like Lancelot when he is held captive by Morgan le Fey, she is willing to die rather than bend, and her virtue grows stronger. At one point she prays, "I yield unto thy will, and joyfully embrace what sorrow Thou wilt have me suffer" (464). Her only plea for herself is that God will "suffer some beam of Thy majesty so to shine into my mind, that it may still depend confidently upon Thee" (464). There is no wavering in her dedication until she thinks of Musidorus, when "pausing awhile" she adds, "And, O most gracious Lord...whatever become of me, preserve the virtuous Musidorus" (464). She can risk her own fortune to God's will, but not her lover's. In the romance tradition, women grow stronger in love as Philoclea has, and men grow weaker, becoming indecisive and ineffective, as Pyrocles does when he assumes his feminine disguise. Although Pamela does not lose her mind like Orlando or Tristan when she thinks of her apparently unattainable love, she does react like a man quailing before an enemy because he thinks of his fair lady and grows weak—another example of one of Sidney's frequent breaks with tradition in his portrayal of female character.

Pamela is strong enough to contain her weakness, however, and forces herself to behave with outward serenity. Cecropia cannot believe that she is much agitated by her captivity because she grooms herself carefully each day and occupies her time reading or doing needlework. Pamela exhibits strict self-control from the outset: "her look and countenance was settled, her pace soft and almost still of one measure, without any passionate gesture or violent motion..." (463). She maintains her control through prayer, demonstrating the most desirable of feminine virtues, piety. Her prayer ("O Lord, I yield unto Thy will and joyfully embrace what sorrow Thou wilt have me suffer") indicates acceptance of God's will, which seems to place her with other stoic heroines who accept passively whatever comes to them. However, when Sidney's narrator describes her he says that "if Philoclea with sweet and humble dealing did avoid their [her captors'] assaults, she [Pamela] with majesty did beat them off" (465). Pamela does not just endure, she actively resists. Since Cecropia controls the castle, Pamela cannot attack her physically; her weapons are words.

Pamela demonstrates her courage when she defends her religion from Cecropia's attack. Pamela has agreed to marry Amphialus if her father gives his permission, knowing that because of the oracle's prophecy he will never permit her to marry anyone. Cecropia knows this too and tries to convince Pamela to marry without permission. Pamela replies that God commands filial obedience from her. When Cecropia presses her, saying that her father is unreasonable and "peevish," Pamela calmly—and with a heroine's conventional piety—replies that her faith in God requires her to obey her father without judging him (487). Cecropia dismisses religion, declaring that it consists of "bugbears of opinions brought by great clerks into the world to serve as shewels to keep them from those faults whereto else the vanity of the world and weakness of senses might pull them" (487). She advises Pamela, "I would not you should love virtue servilely..." (487). She speaks of faith in a divine creator cynically, as foolish superstition:

> Yesterday was but as today, and tomorrow will tread the same
> footsteps of his foregoers: so as it is manifest enough that all things
> follow but the course of their own nature, saving only man, who
> while by the pregnancy of his imagination he strives to things
> supernatural, meanwhile he loseth his own natural felicity. (488)

She follows this explanation with advice for Pamela stemming from her own pragmatic and self-centered creed:

> Be wise, and that wisdom shall be a God unto thee. Be contented, and that is thy heaven: for else to think that those powers (if there be any such) above are moved either by the eloquence of our prayers or in a chafe at folly of our actions carries as much reason, as if flies should think that men take great care which of them hums the sweetest, and which of them flies nimblest. (488)

Pamela cannot maintain her mild demeanor while Cecropia assaults her faith; in striking contrast to the passive figure in the *Old Arcadia*, she lashes out with fierce anger, not caring that her aunt has complete control over her:

> Peace, wicked woman, peace, unworthy to breathe that dost not acknowledge the breath-giver; most unworthy to have a tongue which speaketh against him through whom thou speakest: keep your affection to yourself which, like a bemired dog, would defile with fawning. (488)

This truly is a verbal assault such as no passive, stoic heroine could have uttered. Pamela pounds Cecropia with imperative phrases which call attention to her ascendancy over her aunt and demonstrate her majesty. In calling her "wicked woman," Pamela levels her imperiously and justly, denying her either authority or kinship. When she compares her aunt with "a bemired dog," words that could well provoke a physical attack, Pamela demonstrates complete disdain for her adversary. Cecropia herself indicates that Pamela's words stun her by not attempting to answer them with logic of her own. Pamela's assault and her subsequent use of reason to prove the existence of God win this particular battle, although Cecropia returns to retaliate with beatings and torture. At the moment of Pamela's verbal attack, however, Cecropia slinks off "saying little more unto her but that she should have leisure enough better to bethink herself" (493). Pamela is a most unusual heroine. She exhibits the characteristic masculine virtues listed by Elyot in *The Boke Named the Governour*; she is "fierce, hardy, [and] strong in opinion" (77). She certainly is not the "mild, timorous, tractable, benign" woman he describes as ideal (78).

Pamela is capable of putting aside love to fight with masculine courage even in the enemy's camp.

Pamela's ability to use moral reasoning also sets her apart from silent heroines concerned only to keep their lovers' affections and protect their good names. Neither Sidney's predecessors nor his *Old Arcadia* provides us with a heroine who has the intelligence and the ability to reason through such an argument as Pamela presents to prove the existence of God. She refutes Cecropia's arguments one by one. To Cecropia's claim that "because we know not the causes of things, therefore fear was the mother of superstition," Pamela replies:

> Nay, because we know that each effect hath a cause, that hath engendered a true and lively devotion. For this goodly work of which we are, and in which we live, hath not his being by chance; on which opinion it is beyond marvel by what chance any brain could stumble. For if it be eternal, as you would seem to conceive of it, eternity and chance are things unsufferable together. For that is chanceable which happeneth; and if it happen, there was a time before it happened when it might have not happened, or else it did not happen; and so, if chanceable, not eternal, as now being, then not being. (489)

Pamela proves logically that there is a God, and she concludes with a threat that Cecropia's atheism will bring about her destruction, courageous words from a captive to her captor:

> Since then there is a God, and an all-knowing God, so as he sees into the darkest of all natural secrets which is the heart of man; and sees therein the deepest dissembled thoughts before they be thought; since he is just to exercise his might, and mighty to perform his justice, assure thyself, most wicked woman...that the time will come when thou shalt know that power by feeling it; when thou shalt see His wisdom in the manifesting thy ugly shamefulness, and shalt only perceive him to have been a Creator in thy destruction. (492)

Sidney draws upon longstanding traditions in Christian philosophy to provide
Pamela with her arguments so that her carefully reasoned points resemble those of
such Christian philosophers as Thomas Aquinas. Although his philosophy is not
unusual, Sidney's placement of these ideas, this logical reasoning, in the mouth of
a fictional heroine, is. Most of Sidney's predecessors, including Jean de Meun,
Chaucer, and Ariosto, have their female characters use what wit they possess to
deceive men and get their own way; heroines usually exercise the virtue of silence
to such a degree that even if they could reason morally they would not. In his
development of Pamela as an intelligent, articulate, and vigorously courageous
heroine in the *New Arcadia*, Sidney has truly altered existing perceptions and
stereotypes. When he has Pamela use her mind and her words to attack Cecropia's
atheistic philosophy he also seems to indicate that it is the duty of those who
possess the capacity for moral reasoning to speak out for truth, even if they are
women.

When Cecropia loses the battle of wits to Pamela, she turns to physical
means to bend the princesses to her will, but her efforts only strengthen their
virtue. First she takes servants away from them, thinking them pampered and
unused to wait on themselves; however, Pamela and Philoclea have always taken
care of themselves, since Gynecia did not believe in spoiling her children (another
sign of her wisdom). Next, Cecropia deprives them of good food, giving them only
enough to keep them alive. Finally, she tries torture, even beating them herself
from time to time. The sisters respond to these trials characteristically. Philoclea
cries and asks to be killed quickly, but she has become too strong to grovel; even
in torment her innocence and humility fill her words with gentle dignity:

> If...the common course of humanity cannot move you, nor the
> having me in your own walls cannot claim pity, nor womanly
> mercy, nor near alliance, nor remembrance (how miserable soever
> now) that I am a prince's daughter, yet let the love you have often
> told me your son bears me so much procure, that for his sake one
> death may be thought enough for me. I have not lived so many
> years but that one death may satisfy them. It is no great suit to an
> enemy when but death is desired. I crave but that.... (552)

Philoclea speaks under great duress, but her torture has taught her a measure of self-control. Her speech is neither agitated nor hesitant; a long complex sentence lists all the reasons Cecropia should show her mercy—human decency, the laws of hospitality, womanliness, kinship, and fealty—and interrupts the flow with one parenthetical phrase, her only reference to her present condition. She demonstrates her dignity and sense of self-worth when she claims, "I am a prince's daughter." She uses active voice to remind Cecropia of her youth, "I have not lived so many years...," once more speaking with gentle dignity. Philoclea never once shows any sign of wavering in her resolve; in fact she adds, "As for the granting your request, know for certain you lose your labours, being every day further-off-minded from becoming his wife who useth me like a slave" (552). Although she does not lash out in anger or self-defense, she demonstrates increasing self-control and strength of mind as she endures her torment. She exhibits a softer version of moral courage than Pamela's, but she is no less resolute.

Even under torture, Pamela prefers active resistance to passive acceptance. However, with Cecropia in command, she can only demonstrate courageous self-control; she suffers her torments "with so heavenly a quietness and so graceful a calmness...that while they vexed her fair body, it seemed that she rather directed than obeyed the vexation" (553). This seems to be just the kind of pure and saintly behavior that writers of courtesy books extolled; however, saints used as examples in courtesy books never speak harshly to their tormentors. They suffer humbly and silently, usually until death. Pamela does not practice this virtuous silent suffering. When Cecropia thinks she has brought Pamela to the breaking point and asks her if she is now ready to marry Amphialus, Pamela replies,

> Beastly woman...follow on, do what thou wilt and canst upon me, for I know thy power is not unlimited. Thou mayest well wreck this silly body, but me thou canst never overthrow. For my part I will not do thee the pleasure to desire death of thee: but assure thyself, both my life and death shall triumph with honour, laying shame upon thy detestable tyranny. (553-554)

Unlike Philoclea, Pamela once more verbally assaults Cecropia, insulting her and using sharp forceful sentences like a sword to cut her down. She uses the informal "thou" rather than the more formal and respectful "you" in order to show her disdain and contempt for her aunt (Dobyns 96), demonstrating active, if verbal, resistance and inviting retaliation. It is hard to imagine Chloe or Chariclea or even Bradamante speaking this forcefully and disdainfully to a wicked relative. Before Pamela, silently suffering heroines were the norm.

Sidney never breaks with tradition completely in the *New Arcadia*; Pamela and Philoclea are certainly heroines worthy of their own pedestals. However, Sidney saves them from being plaster saints by allowing them small weaknesses, like Pamela's dithering over her love for Musidorus and Philoclea's untidiness in captivity. They are different from the saintly models drawn for women by his predecessors. They do not endure without question, like Patient Griseldas; they are intelligent creatures capable of rational thought and moral responsibility. While they possess many of the traditional feminine virtues like piety and humility, they also possess many of the virtues often reserved for heroes, like friendship, constancy, loyalty, and personal courage in dangerous situations. The feminine virtues they lack are dutiful, unthinking silence and submission. Philoclea and especially Pamela reach the level of heroes in their mental and moral abilities. Even in his villainesses Sidney breaks with tradition. Cecropia uses no magic powers to prevail in Arcadia; instead she uses the power of her own warped mind. Her evil is not the deviousness usually reserved for women; it is straightforward and pragmatic. Gynecia is perhaps the most unusual woman in Arcadia. Sidney portrays her as neither good nor evil, but as an intelligent and virtuous woman caught up in passion. Sidney's representations of virtues and vices in his female characters indicate that he did not consider these qualities to be gender-specific. He increasingly perceived people as individuals rather than gender stereotypes; that perception made it possible for him to create in the *New Arcadia* new models of female characters that broaden previous concepts of women's capabilities.

NOTES

1 In *Gender and Authorship in the Sidney Circle*, Mary Ellen Lamb notes that men and women probably read the *Arcadia* for different reasons; for women, the Book Three of the revised *Arcadia* provided a model of a "form of heroism appropriate for young women who are under pressure to marry husbands chosen by their parents, and for young brides who are lining in the households of their mothers-in-law" (109). Male readers, on the other hand, "read the *New Arcadia* as a serious work, revealing...insights about...[politics and government]" (112). Men tended to see the female audience as "culpably frivolous and dangerously sexual" (112).

2 Renaissance poetry often expresses the desire for the beloved to have children in order to create images of her/himself, as in Shakespeare's sonnets; a mother does not suggest that the propagation of self-image is the sole reason for motherhood.

3 The most common type of relationship described is the one between servant and mistress, with the servant aiding her lady to find happiness with her lover. The relationship is not a genuine friendship between equals.

4 Sidney's masterly creation of individual speech patterns for his Pamela and Philoclea demonstrates stylistic skill, but it also reveals his powers of observation and his understanding of what today's reader would call human psychology.

5 Lamb notes that Sidney may have modeled Pamela on Protestant martyrs who spoke out about their faith:

> The specific contribution of the Protestant martyr was the authori-
> zation of a model of female heroism enabling speech and even
> rigorous intellectual debate on religious topics. Pamela's impas-
> sioned yet immensely informed and logical arguments against
> atheism owe a debt to this model. (102)

Conclusion

It is impossible to know exactly why Sidney created progressively stronger and more complex female characters throughout his short literary career. The very brevity of that career makes me suspicious of Zandvoort's hypothesis of a simple maturing process (74); it would be highly unlikely, in the late Renaissance, for this process to include a drastic change in attitudes toward women. There was more to it than that. Even in his first version of the *Arcadia*, his creation of Gynecia puts him in advance of other writers of his time in his treatment of women, simply because he displayed her, a lustful woman, with great sympathy and demonstrated that such a woman need not be an evil sinner before she repents or becomes a saint afterwards. More remarkable, in his revision of the *Arcadia*, Pamela and Philoclea have many of the attributes usually reserved for heroes and lack some of those characteristic of heroines. There is no precedent in Sidney's literary antecedents for female characters such as the ones he developed; we must look, instead, to the major influences in his life—his relationship with his queen, his relationships with the women of his family, and his ideology—to find some clue to his creation of his "speaking pictures" of women.

The most problematic of these three influences on Sidney's writing is Elizabeth because she promoted ambiguous images of herself as a woman and as a monarch, and Sidney's reactions to her were ambiguous. Unlike men a generation older than he, Sidney had no problem accepting a female ruler; Elizabeth ascended the throne when he was only four years old. Although female rule was a highly unusual phenomenon in English history, it was the only kind that Sidney ever experienced, and it must have had some influence on him. One might expect that having a woman monarch would alter received notions about women; however, contemporary beliefs about the special qualities of rulers and Elizabeth's manipulation of stereotypes about women may well have nullified any such alterations. Furthermore, Elizabeth's relationship with the Sidney family may have formed his perceptions of her. He certainly did not see her as a saint, but neither was she the opposite. Sidney apparently considered Elizabeth a frustrating, often annoying, woman who yet commanded his respect.

During the Elizabethan period there was a strong belief that God endowed rulers with special qualities which transcended any human weaknesses or disabilities—including the disability of femininity. In other words, even a weak female, as Elizabeth often styled herself, could be used as an instrument of God. By the special grace of God, the people believed, Elizabeth transcended her gender. This idea placed her outside the mainstream of culture; she did not serve as an example for ordinary women. In fact, she exploited her gender, claiming female weakness when it suited her policies (especially in her courtships) and using female stereotypes to her own advantage. This manipulation actually had the effect of reinforcing the existing stereotypes; rather than encouraging her subjects to think of women as capable, intelligent individuals, she really kept alive the belief that they were inferior creatures. In an early speech she called herself "a woman wanting both wit and memory," and mentioned her "fear to speak and bashfulness besides, a thing appropriate to my sex" (in Marcus 138). Antonia Fraser cites another example of her reinforcement of the stereotypes: "Women were popularly supposed to be chatter boxes: when the Queen was congratulated on knowing six languages, she remarked wryly that it was 'no marvel to teach a woman to talk; it were harder to teach her to hold her tongue'" (209). Fraser adds, "She also believed what she said. For she was different. That was the constantly reiterated message" (209).

Leah S. Marcus notes that "Queen Elizabeth presented herself to the nation as both man and woman, queen and king, mother and firstborn son" (137). She adds that Elizabeth "frequently appealed to her composite nature as Queen: her 'body natural' was the body of a frail woman; her 'body Politic' was the body of a king..." (138). In her famous speech at Tilbury she claimed both a woman's physical weakness and a man's courage: "I know I have the body of a weak and feeble woman, but I have the heart and stomach of a king, and of a king of England, too..." (Neale 296). Although she often referred to herself as "Queen," she also styled herself "Prince" and, especially in later years, "King" (Marcus 140). At the same time, she spoke of herself as "virgin mother to her people" (Marcus 142). Elizabeth and her counselors used paradoxes like these to create an aura of myth around the Queen that allowed her to replace Catholic saints in the hearts of her subjects. In *The Cult of Elizabeth*, Strong explains that

> The Cult of Gloriana was skillfully created to buttress public order and, even more, deliberately to replace the pre-Reformation externals of religion, the cult of the Virgin and saints with their attendant images, processions, ceremonies and secular rejoicing. So instead of the many aspects of the cult of Our Lady, we have the 'several loves' of the Virgin Queen; instead of the rituals and festivities of Corpus Christi, Easter, or Ascentiontide, we have the fêtes of Elizabeth's Accession Day and birthday. (16)

Carol Levin explains that Elizabeth "consciously presented herself to her people as a Virgin Queen who could replace the Virgin Mary and help heal the rupture created by the break with the Catholic Church" (97). She deliberately used female stereotypes to portray herself variously as a weak, indecisive woman, a brilliant but unobtainable mistress, and the mother of her people. However, even Elizabeth was not immune to speculation about her chastity. Levin notes that rumors about her sexual activities and possible illegitimate children continued throughout her reign—so that even Elizabeth was a victim of the dichotomous perception of woman as saint or whore (100).

To what extent did Sidney accept the myths that surrounded Elizabeth? How much did she actually contribute to his representation of women? He certainly participated in the pageantry of the court. He probably devised one of the fêtes celebrating the Duke of Anjou's marriage proposal, when the Four Foster Children of Desire assaulted the Fortress of Perfect Beauty, a tower in which Elizabeth sat reigning as "unattainable beauty" (Strong 60). Although Sidney joined the court in such stylized celebrations, he certainly did not worship Elizabeth, or even appear to, as courtiers like Ralegh did. He never addressed so much as a single poem to her. He was almost certainly exasperated because she would not make use of his talents but kept him idling at court (Levy 12). In 1585, when Elizabeth seemed likely to appoint someone else governor of Flushing, he even went so far as to try to sneak away on an expedition with Drake (Wallace 330-331). He also must have been frustrated by her refusal to recognize and reward his family's proven ability in her service. We can understand Elizabeth's distrust of a family which managed to get close to the Protestant Edward VI (Henry Sidney was his intimate companion), then the Catholic Mary (Mary Sidney was her lady-in-waiting and Philip was named for his godfather, Philip of Spain). However, Sidney probably only saw his family's sacrifices for the stability of the kingdom—his mother's beauty marred with the smallpox she contracted while nursing Elizabeth, and his father's long and costly service in Ireland.

Sidney was often at odds with Elizabeth's policies, especially her refusal to join a Protestant league to counter the Catholic strength of Spain and France. His impatience with Elizabeth comes through clearly in a letter he wrote to Walsingham from the Netherlands about Elizabeth's conduct of the war: "If her Majesty were the fountain, I should fear, considering what I daily find, that we should wax dry. But she is but a means whom God useth, and I know not whether I am deceived but I am faithfully persuaded that if she should withdraw herself other springs would rise to help this action" (Wallace 358). Besides revealing his disagreement with his Queen, this letter also demonstrates that Sidney was perfectly capable of seeing her as an instrument of God without believing that she was infallible. A twentieth-century view of Elizabeth's reign reveals that her apparent procrastination was good politics, since she managed to stay out of direct conflict for most of her reign, and she also kept France and Spain from allying against England and other Protestant states. But Sidney could not foresee the outcome, and he was plainly quite irritated by Elizabeth's refusal to act.

His frustration appears in his first fictional enterprise, *The Lady of May*, when he contrasts the active woodsman with the contemplative shepherd, and asks Elizabeth to choose between them. Even though Sidney had loaded the dice in favor of the woodsman, Elizabeth was clever enough to see through his ploy and chose the shepherd. In the *Arcadia*s, the chaos resulting from Basilius' retreat from the world might well signify Sidney's fears for England if Elizabeth did not take a more active role in politics. F. J. Levy notes that Sidney shared "Languet's aggressive Protestantism. And therein he came into conflict not only with...Lord

Burghley, the Lord Treasurer and the Queen's most trusted advisor—but with the Queen herself" (8). Sidney never hesitated to make his disagreement with Elizabeth's policies known.

However, he also expressed a certain admiration for Elizabeth; in the *New Arcadia*, he identifies her with the good Queen Helen of Corinth. Strong notes that Elizabeth's personal colors were black and white (71), the colors Sidney uses for Queen Helen. Sidney describes Helen as "a woman, a young woman, a fair woman" who governs

> A people in nature mutinously proud, and always before so used to hard governors as they knew not how to obey without the sword were drawn; yet could she for some years so carry herself among them that they found cause, in the delicacy of her sex, of admiration, not of contempt: and which was notable, even in the time that many countries about her were full of wars—yet so handled she the matter, that the threats ever smarted in the threateners: she using so strange and yet so well succeeding a temper that she made her people by peace, warlike; her courtiers by sports, learned; her ladies by love, chaste. (351-352)

If this is meant as a favorable description of Elizabeth's reign it may indicate Sidney's respect for her ability—or it may just be a courtly and expedient complement.

I believe that Sidney was indeed influenced by the idea that a prince was God's deputy on earth; this concept was too much a part of his culture, including both Catholic and Protestant theology, for him to be able to ignore it completely. Further, in the controversy that raged about the subject of women as rulers, Calvin declared that "God has at times, for example with Deborah, raised up women of heroic spirit and given them extraordinary grace" (Douglass 96). Even a female prince may serve as God's deputy. But the fact that Sidney criticized Elizabeth in letters about her, and—as when he advised her against the French marriage—to her, indicates that he did not see her as somehow magically transformed by an infusion of grace. Wallace, his chief biographer, says of the letter concerning the French marriage that "Elizabeth had probably never in the whole course of her reign received a letter comparable with this for boldness and frankness of speech" (281). Languet spoke of his admiration for Sidney's "freely admonishing the Queen" (Wallace 220). This admonition is an indication that Sidney saw his sovereign as a fallible human being, one with whom he did not always (or even often) agree. One might imagine that Elizabeth strongly influenced Sidney's portrayal of women, but when one studies Elizabeth's self-portrayal and Sidney's dealings with her, the evidence is inconclusive.

Much more certain is the influence Sidney's mother and sister had on him. The Sidney family seems to have been particularly close; Lady Mary accompanied Sir Henry to Ireland when she was well enough and had no duties at court. James M. Osborne notes that "the affectionate relationship of father, mother, and children is manifest in their letters and other testimony" (5). Unfortunately, most of the correspondence between Sidney and his mother and sister has been lost, discarded, or deemed not important enough to write about, so that we cannot examine his ties with the women in his family very closely. However, there are a few clues to indicate how important those relationships were. One is simply the amount of time they spent together. The Sidney family gathered whenever there was an opportunity. For example, after Philip's sister Ambrosia died in 1575, Elizabeth extended an invitation to his sister Mary to join the court (Waller 13), and the family rejoiced at being able to come together at Kenilworth in July of 1575 during the Queen's progress (Osborne 325, 327).[1] Further, both Philip and Robert chose to spend much of their time with their sister Mary at Wilton. When Mary's son Philip was christened, the whole family took part, with Philip, Robert, and Lady Mary all serving as godparents (Wallace 19). These scanty facts are a small but significant sign of the affectionate bond between the men and women of the Sidney family.

Perhaps one reason that the Sidney women were so much honored in their own family was that Lady Mary's Dudley lineage was more elevated than Sir Henry's. Wallace describes her as probably a well-educated woman, while he laments the lack of evidence: "Unfortunately we have only the most fragmentary information regarding Lady Mary's acquirements, but there is reason to believe that she may have belonged to the group of famous women scholars of her day, among whom her sister-in-law Lady Jane Grey and Queen Elizabeth were conspicuous"

(16). He notes that "Lady Cecil, Lady Bacon and Lady Hoby, three of the brilliant daughters of Sir Anthony Coke, were among Lady Mary's most intimate friends, and we know that she conversed easily in Italian. The scraps of Latin and French in her handwriting in the Sidney copy of Grafton's Chronicle suggest that she had received an education in languages"(17). Wallace gives Lady Mary full credit as "the chief force in shaping his [Philip's] development" (16). She was well-born, intelligent, and capable.

Both Sir Henry and the Queen recognized Lady Mary's abilities. Sir Henry relied on her to represent him at court while he was in Ireland (those times, at least, when she was not in Ireland with him). When Sir Henry was recalled from Ireland in 1578 and Philip was trying to rally support among friends at court, he wrote to his father, "Among which friends—before God there is none proceeds either so thoroughly or so wisely as my Lady, my mother. For mine own part I have had only light from her" (Wallace 200). Again, when Elizabeth intended to elevate Sir Henry's rank without giving him the funds to maintain it, he turned to his wife to be his ambassador in his refusal (Osborne 311). Elizabeth herself made use of Lady Mary's diplomatic abilities in 1559 when she contemplated a Spanish marriage, employing her as an intermediary between herself and the Spanish ambassadors (Wallace 20). Philip must have been constantly aware of Lady Mary's intelligence and ability. Then, too, he knew that his position at court depended more on his mother's Dudley lineage than on the Sidney line. In his reply to an attack on his Uncle Leicester, he answers criticism of the Dudleys' claims to gentility through the female line saying, "these great Honors came to him by his Mother, for these I do not deny they came so; and that the Mother, beeing an Heir, hath been, in all Ages and Contreis, sufficient to nobilitat, is so manifest, that, even from the *Roman* Tyme, in such Cace thei might, if thei listed, an so oftne did use the Mothers Name; and that *Augustus Caesar* had both Name and Empyre of *Caesar*, onely by his Mothers Ryght..." (Collins 64). His very pride in his lineage would make him honor the source of it—his mother.

Sidney's sister, Mary Herbert, the Countess of Pembroke must also have contributed greatly to his ideas about women. Mary Herbert must have been an intellectually stimulating woman. She was educated privately at home, probably at Ludlow or Penshurst, where she "acquired a love for literature, fluency in

English, French, Italian, probably Latin and Greek, and...some knowledge of music" (Waller 12). Margaret Hannay notes that Mary collected books on many subjects—poetry (many in Italian), politics, and history, and that she was also interested in science (*Philip's Phoenix* 48). Philip obviously enjoyed her company; Waller states that Philip was at Wilton in December of 1577 after Mary's marriage to the Earl of Pembroke at the age of sixteen, in 1578 when she was pregnant (and when he probably began his *Arcadia* for her entertainment), and again in 1580 "after the fiasco over Elizabeth's proposed marriage to Alençon and Sidney's rash challenge to the Earl of Oxford....In the next five years, too, although more active politically, Sidney was to return frequently to Wilton, for instance, in 1584, when he started to revise the *Arcadia* and the Apology" (44-45). Whenever he needed a refuge, Sidney turned to Wilton and Mary.

The evidence for Mary's literary ability is in her translation of the Psalms.[2] While there is no indication that she worked with Philip on his translation of the first forty-three Psalms, she did complete the work after his death (Waller 20). Although Ringler considered her revisions of Sidney's poems the work of "an inveterate tinkerer" (quoted in Waller 154), Waller states that "more firmly than her brother, she directed the flexibility, energy, and poetic suggestiveness of the new Elizabethan poetry into the religious lyric....Her poems stand, at their best, as some of the finest contributions to a tradition of religious verse she helped to initiate" (226). After Philip's death, Mary made Wilton a center for literature and learning dedicated to keeping his spirit alive (Waller 17). Her works include translations of *Discours de la Vie et de la Mort* by Phillipe de Mornay, a Protestant writer much admired and also translated by Philip, Petrarch's *Trionfo della morte*, and a play, Robert Garnier's *Marc-Antoine* (Waller 20). Hannay notes that *Marc-Antoine* has a strong political theme; she adds that Mary was "among the first to bring the Continental genre of historical tragedy to England, making her a precursor...[of Shakespeare] and of Jacobean political drama" (*Philip's Phoenix* 129).[3] While she restricted her work primarily to the translations deemed suitable for women, she became the patron for many literary figures, such as Daniel and Nashe (Waller 66, 72), and she "took the unusually aggressive step for an Elizabethan noblewoman to...actually publish some of her own work" (Waller 107). Waller postulates that "the countess was...re-creating in her, perhaps typically English, way a pattern of patronage by noble women that had flourished in Italy and France for a century or more" (39). Although Mary developed her literary talent only after her brother's death, her intelligence and inquiring mind must have made her a model for Sidney's strong and unusual heroines. Perhaps she even encouraged him to move past the stereotypes of women after she read his teasing comments about their nature in his first version of the *Arcadia*, which he wrote for her amusement and at her instigation.

Another important influence on Sidney's concept of women must have been the Calvinist Protestantism which pervaded England from the reign of Edward VI onward. Both Andrew Weiner and Alan Sinfield explain that during Sidney's time there was no official differentiation between Calvinism, or what later became Puritanism, and the Church of England; there were simply more and less zealous Protestants (Weiner 5, 6, Sinfield 12-13). Sidney's group belonged to the more extreme party, which could be identified by "the zeal with which they applied their religious convictions to their daily life" (Weiner 6). Weiner further states that "Sidney and his circle would have seen Calvin as a definitive interpreter of their faith" (8). The precepts of Protestantism practiced in Sidney's England included recognition of the completely sinful nature of mankind, justification by faith rather than by works, and individual responsibility before God—the priesthood of the believer. From this conviction Calvin derived the belief that God has a specific plan for each person, which means that every job at each station in life is a holy calling—the housewife's as well as the statesman's (Douglass 84). The result was intended to be a new kind of freedom for those assured of salvation; there was no longer any need for people to follow rituals or to confess to a priest. This established the primacy of the individual conscience and the need for constant self-evaluation, even for women; all people, regardless of gender, would be held equally accountable before God. The first wave of Protestantism, Luther's, affected the position of women by elevating the status of marriage. Luther held that salvation could only come from God's grace, so the old ideal of celibacy, a form of good works intended to work out the priest's or monk's salvation, gave way to Christian marriage as man's highest condition (Bullough 196). The primary function of women in marriage, however, was still childbearing. Otherwise, Luther accepted the subordinate role of women and firmly denied them any active part in the church (Bullough 199). Later, Calvin further elevated the status of women by changing the concept of women's role in marriage; he taught that "the primary purpose of marriage was social rather than generative....The female had been created as man's inseparable associate in life as well as in the bed chamber" (Bullough 199). In *Women, Freedom, and Calvin*, Jane Dempsey Douglass notes that Calvin constantly stressed the mutuality of marriage. She explains that "Calvin was unusual in the sixteenth century in permitting women equal access to divorce in the case where they have been wronged by adultery and in permitting the innocent partner to remarry" (86). He also allowed divorce for both male impotence and female inability to have intercourse (Wyntjes 173), thus placing equal emphasis on the sexual and generative needs of both men and women.

Calvin also believed that, although men are mentioned more frequently than women in the Bible, the term *men* should be thought of as referring, in most situations, to both men and women (Bullough 199)—a most enlightened view for his time. He could also envision a time when it might be appropriate for women to speak in church. Douglass notes that "commenting on 1 Corinthians 14:34-35, where women are instructed to keep silence in the churches and ask instruction of their husbands at home, Calvin begins by explaining that the chattering of women must have been a problem for the Corinthian church, and so Paul therefore forbids them to speak publicly, either to teach or to prophesy" (52). In making this distinction, Calvin opens the door for women to speak in churches where female chattering is not a problem. He states that women's silence in church is a matter of decorum, not a binding law (Douglass 62); however, he makes it clear that a woman must have a specific call from the Holy Spirit to break this tradition (Douglass 57). Although Calvin's interpretations of some of the more troublesome scriptures concerning women seem to lessen traditional restrictions on their role in the church, he did not emphasize these concepts; one must search for them in his commentaries. These ideas represent more a passive and partial removal of restrictions rather than an active championship of women. Calvinism did not change the situations of most women, but it did encourage men to consider them as individuals who have equal access to God and are responsible for their own consciences.

There is every reason to believe that Sidney was strongly influenced by Calvinism.[4] The Shrewsbury school where he was sent when he was ten years old was run by Thomas Ashton, a zealous Calvinist (F. J. Levy 8). One of the first books Sidney purchased at Shrewsbury was Calvin's *Catechism* (Weiner 8). In fact, the active practice of Calvinism highlights the whole of Sidney's short life. All of his closest ties were with "zealous" Calvinists: his parents, his sister, his uncles Leicester, Warwick, and Huntington, his father-in-law Sir Francis Walsingham, his mentor Languet, and his friends Fulke Greville, John Casimir, and Philip de Mornay (Weiner 7, 8). In later life, Sidney began to translate Philip de Mornay's *A Woorke concerning the trewness of the Christian Religion*, "a Protestant tractate" (Weiner xii). Perhaps the strongest indication of Sidney's personal religious leanings is in his choice of nonconforming Calvinists—Puritans—as his chaplains: "James Stiles, a Puritan lecturer in London whose license to preach was suspended in 1574, became Sidney's chaplain in 1582 and held that post until Sidney's death in 1586. Another of Sidney's chaplains—and one of the two who were present at his deathbed—was George Gifford, a nonconforming minister who was suspended in London in 1584 for publicly refusing to subscribe to Whitgift's...oath" (Weiner 5). Sidney's championship of a Protestant league to the detriment of his political career, his relationships with Languet and other Protestant leaders, and his literary works all affirm his single- minded, sometimes rigid, religious idealism. I firmly believe that Sidney was of the group that "applied their religious convictions to their daily life" (Weiner 6), and that those convictions might well have led him to consider all people—including women—as individuals, not as stereotypical members of a particular group. His rigorous assessment of his Queen may have been the result of his conviction that *all* people, individually, regardless of station or gender, stand equally accountable to God. Perhaps Sidney's belief in the priesthood of each person, along with the Calvinist concept of mutuality of marriage which he witnessed in his own family, led him finally to create complex female characters rather than cultural stereotypes.

Sidney's development of women who are active and strong without being evil or dominant over men was something new in literary history. I find it truly remarkable that Sidney's female characters have for so long taken critical second place to his heroes. The only explanation I can think of is that for so long women in general have been considered less important than men—both in life and in literature. Perhaps because of these cultural idiosyncracies, Sidney's critics—both male and female—have given only cursory attention to his female characters, and thereby have done both themselves and Sidney an injustice. Perhaps the most unusual thing Sidney ever did was to create Stella, Gynecia, Philoclea, and Pamela. In his portrayal of women as intelligent, capable, and morally responsible human beings, Sidney very likely paved the way for writers like Shakespeare who came after him to develop strong active heroines and to alter, however slightly and gradually, cultural perceptions of women.

NOTES

1 It seems to me also significant that Sir Henry erected a "sumptuous monument" to Ambrosia, who was only ten years old when she died (Wallace 148). This might indicate the importance of daughters to the family at a time when daughters were counted inferior to sons.

2 In the past, readers have known of Mary Herbert only through her relationship with her more famous brother. Before 1979, the only major work about her was the biography, *Mary Sidney Countess of Pembroke*, written by Frances B. Young in 1912. Then Gary F. Waller wrote a full-length study of her work in which he states that "Until recently, she has been...the most unjustly underestimated poet of her age" (*Mary Sidney* 275). A new biography of the Countess, *Philip's Phoenix: Mary Sidney, Countess of Pembroke*, by Margaret P. Hannay (1990) re-examines her life and influence, based on account books, diaries, and five previously unpublished letters. Hannay emphasizes Mary Sidney's vital and active role in the Protestant alliance between the Sidneys, Dudleys, and Herberts, her deliberate shaping of Sir Philip Sidney's reputation as a Protestant martyr, and her own literary interests.

3 Hannay suggests that the Countess of Pembroke may have been one of Shakespeare's patrons. She quotes a letter written in 1865 by William Cory, tutor to George, Earl of Pembroke, which says, "we have a letter, never printed, from Lady Pembroke (Mary Sidney) to her son, telling him to bring James I from Salisbury to see *As You Like It*; 'We have the man Shakespeare with us'. She wanted to cajole the king in Raleigh's (sic) behalf—he came" (*Philip's Phoenix* 122). Hannay points out that Mary Sidney's lost letter cannot be authenticated, but that the facts are accurate: "King James I, prevented from entering London because of the plague, spent much of the first autumn of his reign holding court at Wilton....Although there is no record of the play they presented, Shakespeare's company, the King's Men, was paid 30 pounds to perform before the king at Wilton on 2 December 1603, during the period between Relegh's trial on 17 November and the date set for his execution, 13 December" (122-123).

4 Katherine Duncan-Jones speculates that Sidney may have toyed with Roman Catholicism during his youth because of his sympathy for some of the Roman Catholic individuals he knew personally, and because of his family's earlier adherence to that religion. That, of course, is a possibility, but the strong evidence of his early Protestant training and later championship of the Protestant cause lead me to believe that his ideology was firmly Calvinist. Certainly, he was a man quite capable of sympathy for individuals, even though he did not share their beliefs.

Works Cited

Amadis de Gaule. Books 11 and 12. Trans. G. Aubert de Poitiers. Lyons: Francois Didier, 1577.

Ariosto, Ludovico. *Orlando Furioso*. Trans. Sir John Harrington. Amsterdam: Da Capo Press, 1970.

Benson, Pamela Joseph. *The Invention of the Renaissance Woman*. University Park, Pennsylvania: The Pennsylvania State University Press, 1992.

Bornstein, Diane. *The Lady in the Tower: Medieval Courtesy Literature for Women*. Hamden, Connecticut: Archon Books, 1983.

Brundage, James A. "Carnal Delight: Canonistic Theories of Sexuality." Offprint from Proceedings of the Fifth International Congress of Medieval Canon Law, 21-25 September 1976. Citta del Vaticano: Biblioteca Apostolica Vaticana, 1980.

Bullough, Vern L. *The Subordinated Sex: A History of Attitudes Toward Women*. Urbana: University of Illinois Press, 1973.

Castiglione, Baldesar. *The Book of the Courtier*. Trans. Sir Thomas Hoby, 1561. New York: AMS Press, 1967.

Chaucer, Geoffrey. *The Canterbury Tales*. In *The Works of Geoffrey Chaucer*. Ed. F. N. Robinson. Boston: Houghton Mifflin Company, 1957.

————. *Troilus and Criseyda*. Ed. Robert Kilburn Root. Princeton: Princeton University Press, 1954.

Collins, Arthur, ed. *Letters and Memorials of State*. 2 vols. London: T. Osborne, 1746.

Dipple, Elizabeth. "'Unjust Justice' in the *Old Arcadia*. *SEL*, 10 (1970), 83-101.

Dobyns, Ann. "Style and Character in the *New Arcadia*." *Style*, 20 (Spring 1986), 90-102.

Douglass, Jane Dempsey. *Women, Freedom and Calvin*. Philadelphia: Westminster Press, 1985.

Duncan-Jones, Katherine. *Sir Philip Sidney: Courtier Poet*. New Haven: Yale University Press, 1991.

Elyot, Thomas. *The Boke Named the Governour*. Ed. from first edition by Henry Herbert, Stephen Croft. New York: B. Franklin, 1967.

Euripides. *Hippolytus*. In *Euipides I*. Ed. David Grene and Richmond Lattimore. New York: Washington Square Press, 1967.

———. *The Medea*. In *Euripides I*. Ed. David Grene and Richmond Lattimore. New York: Washington Square Press, 1967.

Fienberg, Nona. "The Emergence of Stella in *Astrophil and Stella*." *SEL*, 25 (1985), 5-19.

The Fifteen Joys of Marriage. Trans. Elisabeth Abbott. New York: The Orion Press, 1959.

Fraser, Antonia. *The Warrior Queens*. New York: Alfred A. Knopf, 1989.

Godschalk, William Leigh. "Sidney's Revision of the *Arcadia*, Books III-IV." *Philological Quarterly*, 43 (1964), 171-84.

The Goodman of Paris. Trans. Eileen Power. London: George Routledge and Sons, Ltd., 1928.

Greenfield, Thelma. *The Eye of Judgement: Reading the New Arcadia*. Lewisburg: Bucknell University Press, 1982.

Hannay, Margaret P. *Philip's Phoenix: Mary Sidney, Countess of Pembroke*. New York: Oxford University Press, 1990.

———. *Silent but for the Word: Tudor Women as Patrons, Translators, and Writers of Religious Works*. Kent, Ohio: Kent State University Press, 1985.

Haskell, Ann S. "The Portrayal of Women by Chaucer and His Age." In *What Manner of Woman*. Ed. Marlene Springer. New York: New York University Press, 1977.

Helgerson, Richard. *The Elizabethan Prodigals*. Berkeley, University of California Press, 1976.

Heliodorus. *An Aethiopian History*. Trans. Thomas Underdowne. Intro. Charles Whibley. New York: AMS Press, 1967.

Henderson, Katherine Usher, and Barbara F. McManus. *Half Humankind: Contexts and Texts of the Controversy about Women in England, 1540-1640.* Urbana and Chicago: University of Illinois Press, 1985.

Hull, Suzanne W. *Chaste, Silent and Obedient: English Books for Women 1475-1640.* San Marino: Huntington Liberary, 1982.

Jardine, Lisa. *Still Harping on Daughters: Women and Drama in the Age of Shakespeare.* Sussex: Harvester Press, 1983.

Kalstone, David. *Sidney's Poetry: Contexts and Interpretations.* Cambridge, Massachusetts: Harvard University Press, 1965.

Kelso, Ruth. *Doctrine for the Lady of the Renaissance.* Urbana: University of Illinois Press, 1978.

Lamb, Mary Ellen. *Gender and Authorship in the Sidney Circle.* Madison: The University of Wisconsin Press, 1990.

Lanham, Richard A. *The Old Arcadia* in *Sidney's Arcadia. Yale Studies in English*, Vol. 158. New Haven: Yale University Press, 1965.

———. "Astrophil and Stella: Pure and Impure Persuasion." *ELR*, 1972.

The Laws Respecting Women. Reprinted from the J. Johnson edition, London, 1777. Dobbs Ferry, New York: Oceana Publications, Inc., 1974.

Levin, Carol. "Power, Politics, and Sexuality: Images of Elizabeth I." In *The Politics of Gender in Early Modern Europe.*" Jean R. Brink, Allison P. Coudert, and Maryanne C. Horowitz (eds.) *Sixteenth Century Essays and Studies*, vol. 2. Kirksville, Mo: Sixteenth Century Journal Publ., 1989.

Levy, F. J. "Philip Sidney Reconsidered." *ELR*, 2 (1972), 5-18.

Lindheim, Nancy R. *The Structures of Sidney's Arcadia.* University of Toronto Press, 1982.

Longus. *Daphnis and Chloe.* Trans. George Moore. New York: The Limited Editions Club, 1934.

Maclean, Ian. *The Renaissance Notion of Women.* Cambridge: Cambridge University Press, 1980.

Malory, Sir Thomas. *Le Morte Darthur.* The original edition of William Caxton, rpt. Ed. H. Oskar Sommer. New York: AMS Press, 1973.

Marcus, Leah S. "Shakespeare's Comic Heroines, Elizabeth I, and the Political Uses of Androgyny." In *Women in the Middle Ages and the Renaissance:*

Literary and Historical Perspectives. Ed. Mary Beth Rose. Syracuse: Syracuse University Press, 1986.

Meun, Jean de. *Le Roman de la Rose*, Part Two. Trans. Charles Dahlberg. Princeton: Princeton University Press, 1971.

Montaigne, Michel de. *The Essays of Michel de Montaigne*. George B. Ives, trans. New York: The Heritage Press, 1946.

Montemayor, Jorge de. *Diana*. Trans. Bartholomew Yong. Ed. Judith M. Kennedy. Oxford: Oxford University Press, 1968.

Nichols, John G. *The Poetry of Sir Philip Sidney: An Interpretation in the Context of his Life and Times*. Liverpool: Liverpool University Press, 1974.

O'Connor, John J. *Amadis De Gaule and Its Influence on Elizabethan Literature*. New Brunswick, New Jersey: Rutgers University Press, 1970.

Osborn, James M. *Young Philip Sidney: 1572-1577*. New Haven: Yale University Press, 1972.

Petrarch. *Selected Poems*. Trans. Anthony Mortimer. University, Alabama: The University of Alabama Press, 1977.

Pisan, Christine de. *The Book of the City of Ladies*. Trans. Earl Jeffrey Richards. New York: Persea Books, 1982.

———. *The Treasure of the City of Ladies*. Trans. Sarah Lawson. Middlesex, England: Penguin Books, 1985.

Robertson, Jean. Introduction to *The Countess of Pembrokes's Arcadia (The Old Arcadia)*. By Sir Philip Sidney. Oxford: Clarendon Press, 1973.

Rose, Mark. *Heroic Love*. Cambridge, Massachusetts: Harvard University Press, 1968.

———. "Sidney's Womanish Man." *RES*, 15 (1964), 353-63.

Rowe, Kenneth Thorpe. "The Countess of Pembroke's Editorship of...*Arcadia*." *PMLA*, 54 (1939), 122-38.

Rudenstine, Neil L. *Sidney's Poetic Development*. Cambridge, Massachusetts: Harvard University Press, 1967.

Sannazaro, Jacopo. *Arcadia*. Detroit: Wayne State University Press, 1966.

Sidney, Sir Philip. *The Defense of Poesie*. From *Sir Philip Sidney: Selected Prose and Poetry*, 2nd. ed. Ed. Robert Kimbrough. Madison: The University of Wisconsin Press, 1983.

————. *The Countess of Pembroke's Arcadia* (The Old *Arcadia*). Oxford: The Clarendon Press, 1973.

————. *The Countess of Pembroke's Arcadia* (The New *Arcadia*). Ed. Maurice Evans. Middlesex, England: 1977; rpt. 1982.

————. *Astrophil and Stella*. In *Poems*. Ed. William A. Ringler. Oxford: The Clarendon Press, 1967.

————. *The Lady of May*. In *Prose Works*. Ed. Albert Feuillerat. Cambridge: Cambridge University Press, 1962.

Sinfield, Alan. *Literature in Protestant England 1560-1660*. London: Croom Helm, 1983.

Stone, Lawrence. *Family, Sex and Marriage in England, 1500-1800*. New York: Harper, 1977.

Strong, Roy. *The Cult of Elizabeth: Elizabethan Portraiture and Pageantry*. Great Britain: Thames and Hudson, 1977.

Sullivan, Margaret M. "Amazons and Aristocrats: The Function of Pyrocles' Amazon Role in Sidney's Revised *Arcadia*." In *Playing With Gender: A Renaissance Pursuit*. Ed. Jean R. Brink, Maryanne C. Horowitz, and Allison P. Coudert. Urbana: The University of Illinois Press, 1991.

Terry, Patricia, trans. *Lays of Courtly Love*. Introduction by Charles W. Dunn. New York: Doubleday, 1963.

Tour-Landry, Geoffrey de la. *The Book of the Knight of the Tower*. Trans. William Caxton. London: Oxford University Press, 1971.

Vives, Lodovicus. *The Instruction of a Christian Woman*. Trans. Richarde Hyde. In *Vives and the Renascence Education of Women*. Ed. Foster Watson. New York: Longmans, Greene, 1912.

Wallace, Malcolm William. *The Life of Sir Philip Sidney*. Cambridge: Cambridge University Press, 1915.

Waller, Gary. *Mary Sidney, Countess of Pembroke: A Critical Study of Her Writings and Literary Milieu*. Salzburg: University of Salzburg Press, 1979.

Weiner, Andrew D. *Sir Philip Sidney and the Poetics of Protestantism: A Study of Contexts*. Minneapolis: The University of Minnesota Press, 1978.

Woodbridge, Linda. *Women and the English Renaissance: Literature and the Nature of Womankind, 1540-1620.* Urbana: University of Illinois Press, 1984.

Wyntjes, Sherrin Marshall. "Women in the Reformation Era." In *Becoming Visible: Women in European History.* Ed. Renate Bridenthall and Claudia Koonz. New York: Houghton Mifflin, 1977.

Young, Frances B. *Mary Sidney, Countess of Pembroke.* London: David Nutt, 1912.

Young, Richard B. "English Petrarke: A Study of Sidney's *Astrophel and Stella.*" In *Three Studies in the Renaissance: Sidney, Jonson, Milton. Yale Studies in English*, Vol. 138. New Haven: Yale University Press, 1958.

Zandvoort, Reinard Willem. *Sidney's Arcadia: A Comparison Between the Two Versions.* Amsterdam, 1929.